THE
WOODWRIGHT'S
WORKBOOK

*Merry Christmas
to Ed –
Charles & Nancy, 1987*

THE WOOD WRIGHT'S WORK BOOK

ROY UNDERHILL

The University of North Carolina Press
Chapel Hill and London

© 1986 Roy Underhill

Manufactured in the United States of America

Library of Congress Cataloging-in-Publication Data

Underhill, Roy.

  The woodwright's workbook.

  Bibliography: p.

  Includes index.

   1. Woodwork—Amateurs' manuals.   I. Title.

TT185.U53   1986   684'.08   86-50125

ISBN 0-8078-1711-2

ISBN 0-8078-4157-9 (pbk.)

Original drawings by Kimberly Wagner

Photo credits
Ed Chappell, p. 218
Geary Morton, pp. ii, 108, 115, 116a
Warren Winchester, pp. 223, 224, 225
Perkins Library, Duke University, p. 26
Virginia State Library, Richmond, Va., p. 190
All other photographs, R.E.U.

THANKS

This book is about people, written for all the readers and viewers who have taken the time to put pen to paper. The mail has been arriving at a rate far beyond my ability to respond to each letter individually. In hopes that this will in some way make amends, I dedicate this book to all the people whose letters I have not answered.

This book could not and would not have been written without the help of a lot of folks. My colleagues at Colonial Williamsburg have had to deal with my constant distraction as I devoted my energies to the book and show. Frank Grimsley, Russell Steele, Robert Watson, Ralph Ward, Bill Weldon, Dan Whitten, and Garland Wood—all appear throughout this book, both in the photographs and in their insights.

Thanks to Dan Berg, Roy Black, Mack Headley, George Pettengell, Pete Ross, Dan Stebbins, and George Wilson for their advice and for allowing me to take photographs in their shops. I particularly want to thank Earl Soles, our departmental director at Colonial Williamsburg, for his generosity in providing time and encouragement.

In Williamsburg I have had the advantage of being able to consult busy scholars on a moment's notice. Thanks to Cary Carson, Ed Chappell, John Conlee, Jay Gaynor, Harold Gill, Margie Gill, William Graham, Bob Lyon, and Ray Townsend. Thanks also to Susan Berg and Julie Conlee at the Research Library and audiovisual archivists Suzanne Brown and Rebecca Merck for their invaluable assistance.

This book is graced by illustrations drawn by Kimberly Wagner. She is blessed with patience to match her great talent. I am also indebted to the staff of the photo lab at Colonial Williamsburg. Tom Austin, Brian Exton, Pete Huffman, Noel Perry, Warren Winchester, and their director, Richard McCluney, made my work in the darkroom a lot lighter.

Thanks to Robert Stern and the staff of Old Salem, North Carolina, for allowing me to photograph their unique artifacts and buildings.

It has been a great pleasure to have the help of my brother, Thomas Underhill, in preparing the radiograph that appears in chapter 9. Geary Morton, the director and co-producer of the television series "The Woodwright's Shop," also has several photographs to his credit in chapter 6.

Old friends and new have been there when I needed them—Pat Allen, Fred and Margaret Bair, Charles Hummel, Emil Pollak, and Ken Roberts. Thanks again to Matt Hodgson, David Perry, and the staff of the University of North Carolina Press. I have particularly enjoyed the use of their charge number for the express delivery service.

I have been fortunate to receive some of the best scholarly assistance anyone could hope for. The only weak link is my ability to use their help properly. Any errors or lapses of judgment are solely mine.

"The Woodwright's Shop" began as a series for public television in 1979. The series is produced with contributions from individual viewers, local corporate sponsors, the State of North Carolina, and public television stations throughout the nation. I thank the program managers of these stations for making America safe for serious woodworking comedy.

The personal support and interest of the late Edward B. Rust, Sr., of the State Farm Insurance Companies, our major corporate underwriter, were invaluable in the success of this television series. He was a good friend to us all.

I owe the greatest debt to my family. Jane and the girls have lived for many months on "not until the book is done."

CONTENTS

THE
WOODWRIGHT'S
WORKBOOK

1

THE DEBATE OF THE CARPENTER'S TOOLS

Shall the ax boast itself against him that heweth therewith? or shall the saw magnify itself against him that shaketh it?

—Isaiah 10:15

Annotator's Preface

SLIDE onto a bench here at the Sawyer's Arms. Your brother carpenters have been drinking since before sunset, while you've been out hacking scarf joints in the dark. The veterans from the wars in France have already run out of stories. Give the barmaid a kiss—but check the measure of the cup that she brings. Remember at the pageant last spring? In the play *The Harrowing of Hell,* when all the souls in torment were liberated except one, wasn't it the thieving alewife that Christ left behind?

Ay, now that's better. Another pint of this and you won't care. So what if the taste comes from the stinking Dutch habit of adding hops to the ale, calling it "biere" and pretending to like it, or from the droppings of the pigeons that roost above her brewing vat. Still, another pint of this, and that fool's poem might seem funny tonight. He is so proud of his rhyme that I hear he has even had it written down. Now if only he knew how to read it! Ever since he heard the *Mystery Play of the Nativity* put on by the Wrights of Chester he thinks he can handle verse as well as he can his axe. Yea, but it's true what Joseph of Nazareth said in the play, there's no getting a better life through a carpenter's work.

> With this axe that I beare,
> this perscer and this nawgere
> and hammer, all in fere,
> I have won my meate.
> Castle, tower, nor riche manner
> had I never in my power;
> but as a symple carpenter
> with those what I might gett.

Ah, here he goes. You always hear that a bad workman blames his tools—but bad tools blaming the workman? Well, sit through it one more time. You're bound to think of something to tell your wife when you get home drunk and broke tonight. Besides, five hundred years from now—who's to know?

Note: The verse that follows is adapted from an anonymous fifteenth-century manuscript (copy in the Bodleian Library, Ashmole 61). The original text appears in the appendix of this book.

The "trusty hatchet" is the first to deny the carpenter and his trade. The chip axe is the functional equivalent of our broad hatchet, a "one handed plane-axe, wherewith Carpenters hew their timber smooth" (1611). The word *hatchet* was also common at this time. In the fifteenth-century mystery play *Noah and the Ark*, Cam says, "I have a hatchett wonder keene to bytte well, as may be seene; a better grownde one, as I weene, is not in all this towne." (The "sharper than thou" complex is an ancient one.) Craftsmen hewing to the lines of tradition still prefer the bare blade and "despise the saw and plane as contemptible innovations, fit only for those unskillful in the handling of the nobler instruments."

The argument is joined by the belte, the tree-felling axe. Where the chip axe says that he can do no more than keep the wright from starving, the belte believes that hard work will be rewarded in the end. Specialized forms of the axe serve for everything from tree felling to shaping elaborate scarf joints. Five of the participants in the *Debate* are variants of the axe.

The twybylle, the T-shaped narrow-bladed axe "wherwith carpenters doo make their mortayses" (1584), sides with the chip axe. This contrary fellow's two blades are set at right angles to one another. This would be the picklike, swung version of the two-faced tool, rather than the pushed and levered twivil. In an old German legend, the devil accidentally strikes himself with both ends of this tool on the backswing, making the sign of the cross on his forehead.

The wymbylle is a gimlet, the one-handed borer of little holes and the beginning of bigger things. An insightful theologian wrote in 1643 that "to use force first before people are tought the truth, is to knock a nail into a board, without wimbling a hole for it." The rhyme with thimble is deceptive, as gimlet is seldom so big a bore: "As the wimble bores a hole for the auger." The sound of the word and the plain imagery of the action of this tool made it popular in seventeenth-century writing. We find: "And well he could dissemble, when wenches he would wimble."

A fourteenth-century encyclopedia described how a nephew of the legendary Daedalus "made the first compas, and wrought therwith." Unfortunately, uncle "took greet envie to the childe, and threw hym doun of an highe toure, and brak his nekke." Later, in 1667, Milton wrote of God taking "the golden Compasses, . . . to circumscribe This Universe." Mortal carpenters wield small iron compasses. Large wooden ones usually belong to coopers, for tracing barrel heads. Although builders use compasses, as Joseph Moxon wrote in 1678, to "describe Circles, and set off Distances from their Rule," the compass is also fundamental to the process of "scribing." The compass is drawn along an irregular gap, transferring the contours of one surface to another. When cut to the scribed line, the two pieces fit perfectly together.

The chip ax said unto the wright:
"Meat and drink I shall thee plyght,
But clothes and shoes of leather tan,
Find them where as ere thou can;
For though thou work all that thou can,
Thou'll never be a wealthy man,
Nor none that longs this craft unto,
For no thing that they can do."

"Nay, nay," said the twybylle,
"Unreason is thy only skylle.
Truly, truly it will not be,
Wealth I think we'll never see."

"Wherefore," said the axe/belte,
"Great strokes for him I shall pelte;
My master shall do full well then,
Both to clothe and feed his men."

"Nay, nay," said the compass,
"Thou art a fool in that case.
For thou speaks without advisement;
Therefore thou getyst not thy intent.
Know thou well—it shall be so,
What lightly comes, shall lightly go;
Tho' thou earn more than any five,
Yet shall thy master never thrive."

"Yea, yea," said the wymbylle,
"I am as round as a thimble;
My master's work I will remember,
I shall creep fast into the timber,
To help my master within a stounde
To store his coffer with twenty pounds."

The groping iron is the first "mystery tool" of the *Debate*. One Latin lexicon defined it as the "runcina"—"that tool of the woodworker, graceful and recurved, by which boards are hollowed so that one may be connected with another." A seventeenth-century text states that "grooping is the making of the Rigget [furrow] at the two ends of the Barrel to hold the head in." So a groping iron cut a groove and is a likely ancestor of the cooper's "croze." Medieval rooms were often finished with vertical oak wainscot (split boards) joined by V-shaped tongues and grooves. The tool that cut the groove is no longer known to us, but a "grooving iron" similar to those used until recently in Germany for joining shingles together is the likely descendant of this tool.

Our medieval encyclopedia also credited the invention of the saw to Daedalus's nephew (before he was tossed from the tower for inventing the compass). "This Perdix was sutil and connynge of craft, and bethought hym for to have som spedful manere clevynge of timber, took a plate of iren, and fyled it, and made it toothed as a rugge bone of a fische, and thanne it was a sawe." Saws are difficult for smiths to make. By the seventeenth century, however, Moxon's *Mechanic Exercises* illustrated six varieties of saw, in contrast to the *Debate*'s single reference.

The Daedalus boys don't get credit for the whetstone; the fourteenth-century encyclopedia mentions only that there are "diverse maner of whetstones, and some neden water and some neden oyl for-to whette." The odd early custom of hanging a whetstone around the neck of a liar gets no play in the *Debate*. The 1418 records of the City of London state that "a false lyrer, . . . shall stonde upon the pillorye . . . with a Whetstone aboute his necke." Thomas Tusser advised husbandmen in 1550 to "get grindstone and whetstone for toole that is dull," advice heeded by Powhatan, who asked Captain John Smith for a grindstone in 1607.

Although I have counted the adze as one of the five axe variants in the *Debate*, the difference is more than just the angle of the blade. The adze is rarely used in the full-tilt chopping manner of the axe—except in the rural instance of hollowing mentioned by Tusser: "An axe and an ads, to make troffe for thy hogs." The common carpenter's use is best put by Moxon: "Its general use is to take thin chips off Timber or Boards, and to take off those Irregularities that the Ax by reason of its Form cannot well come at; and that a Plane (though rank set) will not make riddance enough with." In skillful hands the adze is an exceedingly precise tool, the craftsmen holding one end of the work "with the ends of their Toes, and so hew it lightly away."

The file, although not a proper woodworking tool, is the indispensable partner to the saw. Roman files from the first century A.D. were notched near their tang ends for use as wrests for setting saw teeth. Since files must cut other metal, they are the epitome of hardness, as in the 1484 Caxton *Fables of Aesop*—"She [the serpent] fond a fyle whiche she baganne to gnawe with her teethe." Seeing her own blood and thinking it came from the file she bit harder and harder. Moxon mentions that "coarse files" and "most Rasps have formerly been made of Iron and Case-Hardened," rather than from steel. File making is a profession unto itself. Until industrial versions of the automatic file-cutting machine described by Leonardo da Vinci in the sixteenth century were developed, each of the tiny teeth had to be cut with hammer and chisel.

"Nay, nay," said the saw,
"It is but boast that thou dost blow,
For though thou work both day and night,
He will not thrive, I say thee right;
He lives too near the ale-wife,
And for this shall he never thrive."

To him then said the adz,
And said: "Yea, sir, God glads!
To speak of thrift it will not be,
Wealth will our master never see,
For he will drink more in a day
Than thou can lightly earn in twey;
Therefore thy tongue I bid thee hold,
And speak no more words so bold."

The groping-iren then spake he:
"Compass, who hath grieved thee?
My master yet may thrive full well,
How he shall, I will thee tell;
I am his servant true and good,
I assure thee, compass, by the Rood,
Work I shall both night and day;
To get him goods I shall assay."

Then said the whetstone:
"Tho oft my master's thryft be gone,
I shall him help within this year
To get him twenty marks clear;
His axes shall I make full sharp,
That they may lightly do their work;
To make my master a rich man
I shall assay, if that I can."

To the adz then said the file:
"Thou should not thy master so revile,
For though oft he be unhappy,
Yet to his thrift thou shouldst see:
For I think, ere tomorrow's noon,
To earn my master a pair of shoes;
For I shall rub with all my might,
My masters tools to make bright,
So that, within a little space,
My master's purse I shall increase."

The carpenter's chisel is essential for cutting the mortice and tenon joints which are the basis of timber frame construction. Captain John Smith at Jamestowne in 1607 showed his priorities, writing, "As yet we have no houses to cover us, our Tents were rotten, and our cabbins worse than nought: our best commoditie was Iron which we made into little Chisels." These would be poor chisels indeed if they were all iron. Like all the edge tools of the carpenter, they require a steel bit welded to the iron body before they are hard enough to hold an edge. The chisel struck by the mallet gives both power and control, as for sculpture in stone or wood. Yet, as Shakespeare wrote, "What fine Chizzell Could ever yet cut breath?"

The line is spun linen; and the chalk, no more than a chunk of the White Cliffs of Dover. The ancient snap line appears in Odysseus: "Trees then he felled . . . and carefully He smoothed their sides and wrought them by a line." But not even Homer can talk snap lines like Joseph Moxon. "Then with Chalk they whiten a Line, by rubbing the Chalk pretty hard upon it"; then "one of them between his Finger and Thumb draws the middle of the Line directly upright, to a convenient height (that it may spring hard enough down) and then lets it go again, so that it swiftly applies to its first Position, and strikes so strongly against the Stuff, that the Dust, or Atoms of the Chalk that were rubbed into the Line, shake out of it, and remain upon the Stuff. . . . This is called *Lining of the Stuff*."

The pricking-knife leads two lives. It follows the chalkline in the *Debate*, but is a marking tool only in one of its forms. As a scratch awl, the needle point makes indelible guidelines and dots on the wood. As a brad-awl, the end, which resembles a sharpened screwdriver blade, is used to make holes for screws and nails. Forcing it into the wood with the blade oriented across the grain, the craftsman then repeatedly twists it to push the wood aside. According to Moxon, the "Pricker Is vulgarly called an Awl: Yet for Joiners Use it hath most commonly a square blade, which enters the Wood better than a round blade will; because the square Angle in turning it about breaks the Grain, and so the Wood is in less danger of splitting."

The piercer is today's brace and bit, one of the four boring tools of the *Debate*. Two of them appear in the fifteenth-century Chester mystery play: "With this axe that I beare, This percer, and this nawger. . . ." Theory has it that the piercer/brace was introduced into Europe by returning Crusaders, for it appears suddenly in the early fifteenth century with no discernible European ancestors. The significance of this tool is that it uses full rotary motion, rather than the intermittent or reciprocating motion of the other tools. The next logical woodworking step for this crank action is credited to Leonardo da Vinci, who applied it to spinning the flywheel of a lathe. From this it was a simple progression to the increasingly complex and powerful mechanisms of industry. I am glad that Moxon illustrated this tool because in his text one finds the historian's booby prize: "Its Office is so well known, that I need say little to it." He does caution that "you must take care to keep the Bitt straight to the hole you pierce, lest you deform the hole, or break the Bitt" and that "you ought to be provided with Bitts of several sizes, fitted into so many Padds." The "padds" are the tapering square wooden shanks fitted to the ends of each bit. The padd, in turn, fits into a corresponding socket on the brace.

Than said the chisel:
"If he ever thrive, he bears him well;
For though thou rub till thy head ache,
His wealth from him it will be take:
For he loves good ale so well,
That he therfore his head will sell:
For he some days seven pence will drink;
How he shall thrive I cannot think."

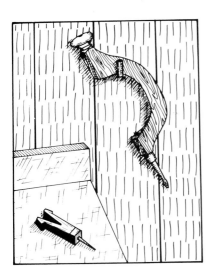

"Yea, yea," said the line and the chalk,
"My master is like too many folk;
Though he love ale far too well
To thrive, and this I shall him tell;
I shall mark well upon the wood,
And keep his measures true and good,
And so by my measures all,
To prosper well my master shall."

Than bespake the prykyng-knife:
"He lives too nigh the ale-wyfe;
She makes oft-times his purse full thin,
No penny sometimes she leaves therein.
Tho' thou get more than other three,
Wealthy man he can not be."

"Yea, yea," said the piercer,
"That which I say it shall be sure;
Why chide ye each one with another?
Know ye not well I am your brother;
Therefore none contrary me,
For as I say, so shall it be.
My master yet shall be full rich;
As far as I may reach and stretch,
I will him help with all my might,
Both by day and by night,
Fast to run into the wood,
And bite I shall with mouth full good,
And this I swear, by my crown,
To make him sheriff of the town."

What tool has a more wondrous name than the skantyllion? "And do we well and make a tower, With square and scantilion so even, that may reache heigher than heaven" (1300). It is no accident that the scantillion is paired with the square in this quotation, because they are used together in truing rectangular stock. The scantillion is the equivalent of the modern gauge, used to scribe a line parallel to an opposing surface. Stock so prepared is termed "scantling." Thus, we have from 1556 *The Spider and Flie*: "Whiche sqwyre shall sqware me, a scantlin well bent, For a right rewle, to show me innocent."

The crow is an odd bird for a simple lever. Crows have been recovered at Pompeii, some with claws and some without. Over the centuries this tool appears to have been used more for moving than nail pulling. In the mid-sixteenth century, folks called for "longe crowes of iren to lyfte great burdens." Later that same century, a player in Shakespeare's *Comedy of Errors* said, "Well I'll breake in: go borrow me a crow." (Which is also one of the earlier references to the great tradition of borrowing tools, and probably explains why the hammer is not present at the *Debate*.) A century later, Moxon illustrated a crow with a claw, but says only that they are to be thrust under the "the ends of great, heavy Timber" to lift them to put a roller underneath. No mention whatever of pulling nails.

Perhaps this is the same rule that was missing a century later at the Globe Theatre performance of *Julius Caesar*.

> *Flavius.* Speak, what trade art thou?
> *Car.* Why, sir, a carpenter.
> *Marullus.* Where is thy Leather Apron, and thy Rule?

Had this scene actually happened in ancient Rome, the tool in question might well have been a foot-long bronze folding rule divided into twelve "unciae," from which we derive our "inch." But Shakespeare wrote with his own time in mind. Thus, the rule might have been a larger and more conspicuous, ungraduated straightedge—or even the proverbial "ten-foot pole" described by Moxon for laying out house frames and ground plots. This rule makes here an early reference to "dying like a dog."

Shakespeare's Roman carpenter of two thousand years ago may also have carried a plane that could easily be mistaken for those used less than two hundred years ago. Planes recovered in Pompeii are beautifully made of wood, soled with iron. Curiously, although planes appear in many illustrations from the Middle Ages (usually of the Holy family or of Noah building his ark of "timber, i-planed wel smethe"), no planes are known to have survived from this time. The plane from the *Debate* offers to "cleanse on every side." Such carefully prepared stock reaches into the realm of the joiner, as distinguished from that of the carpenter. The distinction of the joiner's trade did exist at the time—one of the laws of Henry VIII applied to persons using "any of the misteries . . . of smithes, joigners, or coupars."

"Soft, sir," said the skantyllion,
"I think your luck be nearly done;
Ever so cruel thou art in word,
And yet thou art not worth a turd!
For all the good that thou get might,
He will spend it in one night."

Then the crow began to speak,
As if his heart was like to break,
To hear his brother so reviled,
And said: "Thou speaks like a child;
Tho' my master spend ever so fast,
Enough he shall have at the last,
Fortune he'll have as much as they,
That drank not a penny till their dying day."

"Yea, yea," said the Rule
"In faith, thou art a fool,
For, if he dies and has right nought,
Who trusts that thou will give him ought?
Thus shall he lie upon the ground,
And be buried like a hound:
For, if a man have ought before,
When he has need, it is good store."

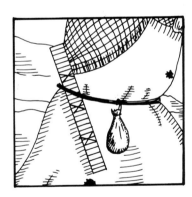

"What, sir rule," said the plane,
"Another reason I will thee say;
Tho oft my master have no stock,
Yet thy master thou should not mock;
For yet a means I shall see,
So that my master shall prosperous be.
I shall him help, both day and night,
To get him good with all my might,
I shall cleanse on every side
To help my master in his pride."

If it were not already apparent that the *Debate* is the work of a carpenter rather than a poet, this verse should make it plain. The fraternity of the broad axe and the plane is obvious only to one who is familiar with the process of hewing timbers. Most of the roundness of the log is generally chopped from the log with the same sort of axe used for tree felling; the broad axe only carefully slices off the last of the roughness. But the broad axe does indeed look like a powerful weapon. For countless years, as in a fourteenth-century poem, men have gone "to batail . . . With brade ax, and with bowes bent."

The twyvette and the twibill are often considered to be one and the same tool. Their appearance together in the *Debate* shows their individuality. The word *twivil* survives as the name of a two-headed morticing knife that is pushed and rocked, rather than swung like an axe. Both ends of a mortice are bored through with an auger and the wood between ripped out with the twivil. The larger version is a proper carpenter's tool and measures over four feet long; it uses leverage rather than velocity to attain its power. The broad chisel end of this tool is sharpened on the sides as well as on the end, so that it can cut as it levers against the top end of the mortice. In France, they are called *besaiguë* and are used with "*beaucoup d'art*." These tools are much more common on the continent of Europe than in England. However, the Hundred Years War with France (Joan of Arc, etc.) had just ended, and it is no surprise to find French influences in the fifteenth-century English tool kit.

The block and tackle were well known to the ancient Greeks and Romans. They also knew the technique of combining them to multiply their power, and understood that "as in the lever, time is lost as power is gained." Pulleys from the Tudor warship the *Mary Rose*, which capsized off Portsmouth, were splendidly preserved in the mud. Like most tools of the carpenter, pulleys are made by a specialist. A 1568 church account notes payment "to William, torner, for turnynge of the powleys." Pulleys are essential to the carpenter raising a heavy oak timber frame. A scene from 1577 would be familiar to anyone of an agricultural persuasion: "They have a Pully . . . wherwith they hoyse up the Corne to the very Rafters of the house."

A windlass is but a lever acting on a rope, which, in combination with the block and tackle, is capable of exerting tremendous force. Chaucer tells in the "Squire's Tale" of a brass horse fastened to the ground so hard that "ther may no man out of the place it dryue For noon engyn of wyndas ne polyue." The familiar windlass is used for high lifting building materials as a structure rises—and for wells and mines where "with a wyndeles turned by fowre men they drawe vpp the coales" (1603). Horizontal pulling, however, is more commonly handled by a capstan, or "crab," with the rope winding on a vertical shaft. In 1586, forty capstans, each turned by twelve men and two horses, were employed to raise a 327-ton obelisk at the Vatican.

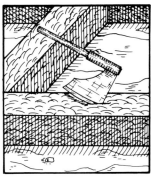

The broad ax said withouten miss,
He said: "The plane my brother is;
We two shall cleanse and make full plain,
That no man shall us gainsay,
And get our master in a year
More silver than a man may bear."

"Nay, nay," said the twyvette,
"Wealth I swear be from you fetched,
To keep my master in his pride;
In this country ye can not abyde,
Unless ye steal and be a thief,
And put many men to grief:
For he will drink more in an hour
Than two men may earn in four.
When ye have wrought all that ye can,
Still shall he never be a wealthy man."

Then be-spake the pullyff,
With great strong words and stiff:
"Hold, sir twyvette, me think you grieved;
What devil hath you so deceived?
Tho oft he spend more in a year
Of gold and silver than thou may bear,
I shall him help with all my might;
I hope to make him yet a knight."

"What, sir," said the windlass, "rule,
Me thinks thou art but a fool;
For thou speaks out of season,
It will not be, by simple reason;
A carpenter to be a knight?
That was ever against right;
Therefore shall I tell thee a saw,
'Who would be high - shall be brought low.'"

Another mystery tool. What could a rule-stone be? We already have a rule. Could that be an unmarked straightedge, and this the one that bears the measurements? But why separate rules, and why a stone? There are three clues that point to the most likely identity of this "true man." The first clue is the material—stone. Second, is the line "as I am a true man" and, third, is the absence of an essential carpenter's tool from the *Debate*. Always, "the carpenter hath his squyre, his rule and his plummet" (1553). The plummet is the plumb bob, essential to bring a structure to vertical. A plumb bob is a "true man" and, although usually made of lead, could well be stone. In any case, the rule-stone makes here the first recorded use of the expression "to rule the roost."

"The gouge" says Moxon "is a Chissel having a round edge, for the cutting such Wood as is to be Rounded, or Hollowed." One of the hollows that a carpenter needs is the shallow round pocket required to start a shell auger into the wood. Otherwise, the screwless, pikeless auger wanders about on the surface and never takes hold. More important, though, is the relationship of the gouge to the quality of fifteenth-century carpentry work. Many of the exposed timbers were being elaborately moulded and carved. The "scribing" gouge, with its bevel on the concave surface, allows such beams to be precisely fitted where they intersect. This produced expensive looking work—which often concealed inferior joints that soon failed. Carpenters were forced by the pressure of the market to cheat where it would not show.

Ropes and cables are vital to mariners, "from the anker he cutteth the gabyll rope" (1523), and builders, "at the west ende of Powlles stepull was tawed a cabell roppe" (1556). Both entrust their lives to the skill of the roper. Until recently, every community had a rope walk, just as it had a mill and a church. His waist encircled with raw hemp or flax, the roper walked slowly backwards, feeding more fiber into the lengthening yarn, which was twisted by a hook spun by his co-worker. Two of these yarns twisted together make the strands which are in turn twisted together to make a rope. When three of these ropes are twisted together, one has made a proper cable-rope. It hardly matters, but it was originally a cable, rather than a camel, that had such little chance of passing through the eye of a needle. Carpenters, however, are seldom denied passage through the Gates of Heaven on the basis of excessive wealth.

Ah, the wife. Fifteenth-century girls married who their families told them to. The idea was to unite for advantage and not for emotional attachment. Henry VIII had yet to get the divorce business under way, but husbands died earlier than wives, and after her first marriage a woman could do as she pleased. With a few years of "good marrying and fortunate dying," a woman could rise to the top of society, or even marry for love. The wife of this drunken carpenter might await just such an opportunity.

This constant guide to the angle of rightness is so characteristic of the wright's craft that from ancient times, as in the fifteenth century, "the carpenters ben signefyed by the dolabre or squyer."

The gouge said: "The devil's dirt
For anything that thou can work!
For all that ever thou can do,
It is not worth an old shoe.
Thou hast been apprentice these seven year
And still thy craft have yet to learn;
If thou could work as well as he,
Our master's wealth shall never be."

Then spake the wright's wife:
"Neither of you shall ever thrive,
Neither the master, nor the men,
For nothing that ye do can:
For he will spend within a month
More wealth than any three men hath."

"Yea," then said the rule-stone,
"My master hath many foes;
If ye would help him at his need,
Then my master should succeed;
But what so ever ye bragg or boast,
My master yet shall rule the roost:
For, as I am a true man,
I shall him help all that I can."

"Soft, sir," said the cable-rope,
"Methinks good ale is in your tope;
For thou speaks as thou would fight,
And would, if thou had any might.
But I shall tell thee another tale,
How my master I shall avail;
Haul and pull I shall full fast
To raise houses, while I may last,
And so, within a little throw,
My master's wealth shall surely grow."

The square said: "What sey ye, dame?
Ye should not speak my master shame."

Spinning yarn from wool or flax was but the most common of the trades practiced by women. Brewing was traditionally dominated by women, as was the English industry of producing cloth from imported raw silk. A merchant's wife could farm out work in the community and end up running a large business on her own. Women were active as corn wholesalers, worked in manual trades, and stood ready to continue their husbands' businesses. One popular medieval legend concerns a blacksmith who was ordered to make the nails for the crucifixion. When he pretended that his hands were injured and that he could not work, his wife quickly stepped in to do the job.

Tudor masons, too, used the square as their symbol. "I beseech you, that the stone is to be fitted to the square, not the square to the stone" (1618). A mason's square is more likely to be iron than is a carpenter's. The wright's square has a thick body, or beam, to catch on the side of the work, and a thin tongue, or blade, to stretch across it.

This debate between the defeatist faultfinders and the optimists is fueled by the valid points of both sides. Even though their power was waning, the local "guilds merchant" could still set standards for wages and quality control. Artificially low prices for fancy work forced builders to concentrate on the "skin" while skimping on the "bones" of their work. Thus a man must "steal and be thiefs." A craftsman could rise to wealth and power, not by the skill of his hands, but by connections and by increasingly controlling the labor of others. Enough to drive a man to drink.

Draught-nayle? Moxon called this tool the hook-pin. It is the carpenter's equivalent of the machinist's tapered drift-pin used to force two holes into alignment. "Its Office is to pin the Frame . . . together, whilst it is framing, or whilst it is fitting into its Position. . . . These drive into the Pin-holes through the Mortesses and Tennants," and, being tapered, pull the joint together. The carpenter will then "strike under the Hook, and so knock it out. Then if the Frame lie in its place, they pin it up with wooden Pins." In the *Debate*, as in the construction of a timber frame, it is the draught-nayle that brings the opposing sides together into a new alignment, placing the blame squarely on the carpenter's defenders.

The wage of seven pence a day is high. The fifteenth-century journeyman carpenter could expect six pence a day for summer work. This day began at 5 o'clock in the morning and lasted until around seven in the evening. The day was punctuated with a half hour for breakfast and an hour and a half for midday dinner and a nap. Winter work went from "can't see" to "can't see" (dawn to dusk), and the pay was correspondingly less. There were quite a few saint's days and festivals and market days, and work did end at about five o'clock on Saturdays. So in spite of the long hours, the carpenter's life left him ample time to drink his pay.

"Square, I have no other cause,
I swear thee, by Saint Eustase:
For all the yarn that I may spin,
To spend at ale he thinks no sin.
He will spend more in an hour,
Than thou and I can get in four."

"Mary, I shrew him and thee too,
And all them that do as ye do:
For his servant I trust thou be,
Therefore gain thou'll never see;
For if thou learn that craft from him,
Thy wealth I swear shall be full thin."

"Yet me thinks ye be to blame
To give my master such a name:
For tho' he spend more than ye have,
Yet his worship ye should save."

The draught-nail then spake he,
And said: "Dame, that is no lie,
Ye know the manner of these freaks,
That thus of my master speaks;
But listen to me a little space,
I shall now tell thee all the case,
How they work for their good,
I will not lie, by the Rood!
When they have worked an hour or two,
At once to the ale they will go,
And drink and toast there constantly:
'Thou to me,' and 'I to thee.'
And one says, 'The ax shall pay for this,
Therefore the cup once I shall kiss';
And when they come to work again,
The belte to his master will this say:
'Master, work us not out of reason,
The day is very long of season;
Small strokes let us slowly hack,
And sometimes let us ease our backs';
The wymbulle speaks softly, 'Ah, sire,
Seven pence of a day is small hire

For wrights, that work so fast,
And in our work have great haste.'
The groping iren then says full soon:
'Master, want ye this work well done?
Let us not work until we sweat,
For catching of over great heat.
For we may happen after cold to take,
Then one stroke may we not hack.'
Then be-spake the whetstone,
And said: 'Master, we want to go home:
For fast it draws unto the night;
Our supper by now I know is dyght.'
The line and stone, the piercer and file,
Say 'That is a good council!'
The crow, the plane, and the square,
Say, 'We have earned well our hire!'
And thus with frauds and falsehood
Comes many a true man to no good.
Therefore, by all that I can see,
They shall never thrive nor wealthy be;
Therefore this craft I will go fro,
And to another will I go."

Then answered the wife in hye:
"If I might, so would I,
But I am to him bound so fast,
That off my halter I may not cast;
Therefore the priest that bound me apprentice
He shall truly have my curse,
And ever he shall have, til I die,
In whatever country that he abide."

Therefore, wrights, take heed of this,
That ye may mend what is amiss,
If truly that ye do your labor
For that will be unto your honor;
And greeve you nothing at this song,
But ever make merry your selves among.
And not at him that it did make,
No envy of him should ye take,
Nor none of you should do him blame,
Because the craft hath done him shame.

2 WORKBENCH

Here is a good hacckinge stoccke;
on this you may hewe and knocke.

—Mystery Play of Noah's Ark, fifteenth century

H o w would you fit boards tightly together if you did not have a woodworking plane?

You might use an adze or hatchet—first scribing the joint with a compass or overlapping the boards and marking them with a scratch awl. Or you might rub one of the surfaces with charcoal and then press it against the other. Then you would chop only the marked areas, repeating the process by trial and error until the surfaces were perfectly fitted together.

You could also fit them by repeatedly running a saw kerf down the imperfect junction. This would subtract from each surface only in the places where the boards were closely abutted. Where there were gaps, the saw would pass along without making any impression. When the saw teeth cut both surfaces along their whole lengths the two pieces should fit perfectly. A sawhorse or two would be all that you needed.

The alternative to custom matching the serendipitous contours of the boards, each to the other, is to bring all surfaces to the one shape that will match any other like itself. You sacrifice individuality for the convenience of this abstract constant. The solution, in both senses, is the plane.

But, since the glory days of Rome, when the woodworking plane appeared, working with planes has meant working on a suitable bench—not just to provide a flat, elevated surface but to somehow hold the work so that both hands are free to use the plane. To enter the era of modern joinery, you must have both planes and a bench to use them on.

CLAVES AND MORTICING STOOLS

The road from chopping block to joiner's bench has many stops along the way. Other woodworking operations besides planing need the work to be held more solidly than under foot, knee, or derriere. Wooden shoe makers and pulley block makers both use augers and gouges in their work. And both use a heavy, four-legged bench called by the block makers, a clave. The strength of the clave is its simplicity. Basically, it is no more than a log with a big notch in the top where you place the work. Wedges driven between the work and the end walls of the notch lock everything in place.

Chairmakers use low, heavy benches to hold pieces as they shape them and cut the joints in them for assembly. The bench illustrated in 1775 by the French master woodturner Hulot is basically the same as those still used by Windsor chair makers in England and by rural craftsmen in Appalachia. This bench differs from the clave in that the work is wedged lengthwise between pegs set into the level top. It has the additional advantage of allowing the chairmaker to sit straddling the bench as he works.

Hulot's bench also accommodates the shaving of long pieces with a drawknife. The drawknife, like the plane, requires the free use of both hands. Thus, as Joseph Moxon wrote in 1678, workmen "set one end

[above]
French sabot *makers in Diderot's eighteenth-century* Encyclopédie *(1763).*

[opposite]
The joiner's bench. Robert Watson making a sash for Anderson's forge.

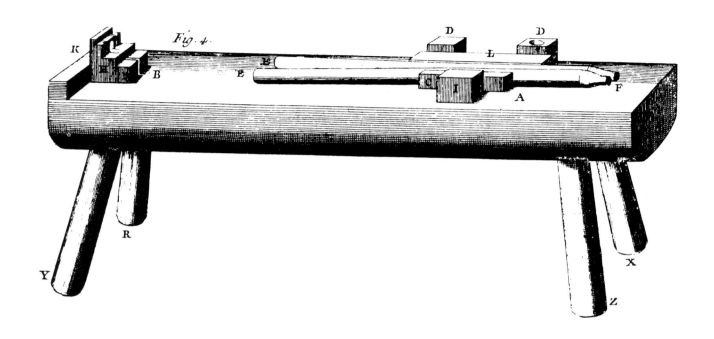

[above]
*The ubiquitous chairmaker's framing
bench, as shown by French woodturner
Hulot in 1775.*

[below]
*The shaving horse in 1556 (Agricola,
De Re Metallica).*

of their Work against their Breast, and the other against their Work-bench, . . . and so pressing the Work a little hard . . . keep it steady in its Position." The Hulot bench allows the worker to sit as he shaves, one end of the work set against the block on the end and the other against a wooden breastplate. (This breastplate, incidentally, also served as the head of the bit braces used to bore the holes for chair framing and was regarded as something of a badge of office in English chairmaking districts.)

SHAVING HORSES

Breastplates and notched benches are all right, but for true drawknifing pleasure, nothing beats the shaving horse. One of the earliest representations of this bench appears in the 1556 German metallurgy book by Agricola, *De Re Metallica*. Here, the craftsman is pictured using it to shave "fuzz-sticks" which will burn hot and fast down in the mines. This is hardly a sophisticated use of this device; yet perhaps it is no accident that Agricola shows it in front of a shingle-covered structure. Holding shingles for shaving is its traditional assignment, as in the 1845 American novel *Margaret* in which, amid a "pile of fresh, sweet-scented white shavings and splinters," sits "a draw-horse, on which Hash smooths and squares his shingles."

A shaving horse, or any bench, works well only if it fits the person who is using it. French woodworker Roubo, in his 1775 discussion of the shaving horse, relates how they must be made larger or smaller for those who are "*plus grandes*" or "*plus petits*." They should be proportioned so

The horse in 1775 (Roubo, L'Art du Menuisier*).*

Virginia shaving horse in the room where Stonewall Jackson died (photograph ca. 1863).

that "at the start of the stroke, your arms should be stretched, but not stiff, and at the end of the stroke, your body should always stay in balance, and therefore, always in command."

THE PLANING BENCH

What's good for a drawknife is not so good for a plane. The planing bench is intended to support the work at a convenient height for planing, around 30 inches or so. But the basic units of joinery and cabinetmaking are boards—which are long, wide, and thin. What works to hold the narrow face at the proper height will not do for the wide face. The basic joiner's bench has two arenas of board holding, one on the front to work the edges and one on the top to work the broad faces. The evolution of the joiner's bench is essentially the increasing sophistication of the mechanisms for holding the work in these two positions.

HOLDFASTS AND HOOKS

Even the most basic bench, just four legs and a top, becomes wonderfully versatile when provided with stops and holdfasts. The end of the board that you are planing simply needs to hit against something to keep it from shooting off the end of the bench. On the top, this is usually a toothed iron set into a wooden shaft running stiffly in a mortice through the bench top. Earlier stops were pounded directly into the bench top—even

Hammering locks the holdfast in its oversized hole in the bench top.

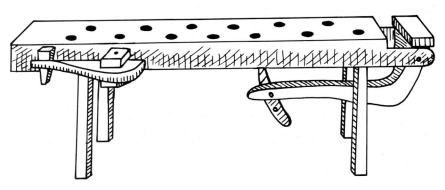

Joiner's bench from Estonia uses levers rather than screws to operate its two vises (after Viires, Woodworking in Estonia, 1960).

a big nail will do. This stop is customarily set through the left front corner of the bench, to accommodate the right-handed majority. No one could mistake the meaning of a 1777 *Virginia Gazette* advertisement which described a runaway slave "named Harry, . . . by Trade a Cooper and Carpenter, when he works at a Bench, he works at the wrong end."

The hook on the front needs a different configuration from the one on top. This stop must act like a crevice to hold the board tight up against the front of the bench. The board must also be supported underneath by pegs which may be placed any of the vertical array of holes provided to suit boards of differing widths. Because boards are different lengths as well, these holes can be placed all along the bench front, or they may be a single row on a vertical member which slides on tracks down the length of the bench.

These holes on the front of the bench, and others in the top, may also serve as lodgements for that remarkable device, the holdfast. When this simple L-shaped iron is set with its long arm loosely in a hole and the short arm on the work, a single blow with the mallet will cause it to become cocked in the hole—as tight and secure as if it were bolted. A single strike on the back releases its grip. Its one disadvantage when used on top of the bench is that it intrudes on the very surface which you want to work. Small trouble when morticing, but always in the way of the plane.

SCREW VISES

The bench illustrated by Moxon in 1678 is an ordinary hook and hold-fast model, with the clumsy addition (obviously an afterthought) of a double screw vise tacked on to the right front. As the ability to make wooden screws and the means to afford them grew in the eighteenth century, they slowly began to appear on workbenches. This represented a return to the notch and wedge of the blockmaker's clave, except now the wedge was wrapped around a cylinder. The double screw front vise was used on both of the large benches owned by the eighteenth-century cabinetmaking family, the Dominys of Long Island. These beautifully simple benches and some of the furniture produced on them may be seen today at the Winterthur Museum in Wilmington, Delaware.

Two other types of front screw vises are the parallel bar type shown in Peter Nicholson's 1812 *Mechanic's Companion* (a remake of Moxon's *Mechanick Exercises*) and the vertical jaw vise illustrated by Roubo (and used on my own bench). Though written half a century earlier than Nicholson's, Roubo's book described an innovation that, in much of the world, eventually became the standard on the woodworker's bench.

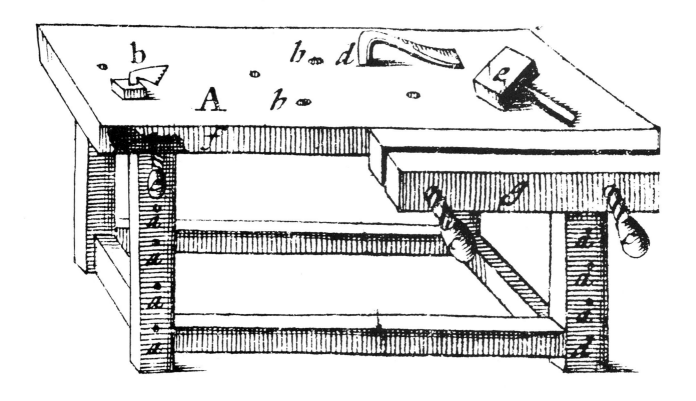

THE END VISE

Moxon's bench from 1678 (Mechanick Exercises).

"Eventually" is the key word here. Over forty years later, in 1816, Roubo's countryman Bergeron would write that the end vise was still not common in Paris, even though "this ingenious device gives the advantage of enabling one to work on three faces of the clamped work." The end vise does this by pinching the board between two stops on the bench top, eliminating the intrusion of the holdfast. Bergeron also appreciated the opening of the end vise "to hold a piece perpendicularly. Cabinetmakers use it for sawing sheets of veneer, straight and mitred tenons, and for clamping small pieces after gluing."

These benches with end vises are commonly called "German benches," because, according to Roubo, "either it was invented in Germany or, which is more likely, by the German cabinetmakers, which are numerous in Paris." There are occasional assertions that this form was known in Germany as a "French bench" (in the sort of extra-national attribution usually reserved for social diseases). In any case, it has always been more popular on the continent of Europe—and in melting-pot America—than in Britain.

Roubo's German bench has the usual vise on the front, with an adjustable bottom strut to keep the jaws parallel on different sizes of work. It also has an unusual second vise that slides in tracks. Its legs, which are

[right]
Nicholson's bench from his 1812 Mechanic's Companion.

[below]
A copy of the Nicholson bench at the Anthony Hay shop in Colonial Williamsburg.

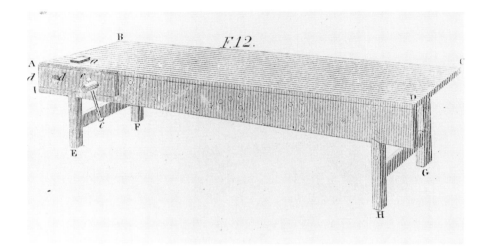

morticed only three-quarters of the way through the thickness of the top, are superior to those of common benches, which, he noted, are morticed "all the way through, because it is the custom."

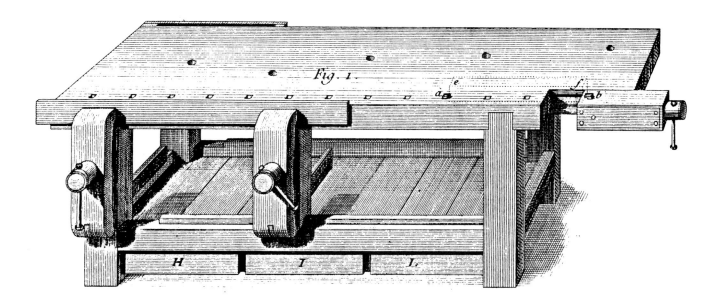

[above]
Roubo's "German" bench from the 1770s carries the new vise on its right end.

[left]
A sophisticated Moravian bench with characteristic tusk tenons at Old Salem, North Carolina.

THE HARD PLACE

The common thread in all of these benches is solidity. Energy expended in deformations of the bench is wasted. You cannot work long or well at a bench that flexes under the passage of the plane or that bounces under the blows of the mallet. The big bench in the Dominy shop stands 29½ inches tall on 4 by 4 legs. The top, excluding the 10-inch-wide back shelf, measures 12 feet long, 17½ inches wide, and over 5 inches thick— a single piece of oak for generations of work.

"He that will a good bench win must split thick and hew thin."

[opposite]
A bench top supported by a frame all around can be made thinner than those on four legs.

THE TOP

Enough history; now let's consider a bench for your own shop. The ancient bench top was a single massive timber. You can cut a big tree, hew it rectangular, and saw it in half, making two bench tops. The sawn, heart side of the timber goes up and the hewn surface goes down. The heart face can be harder than the bark face, and the slight crowning that will happen as it seasons can be less troublesome than the hollow warping of the other face. Flaws, such as rotten knots, may determine which face you must use. The benches in the Dominy shops are oak; many makers use beech or elm, and hard maple or birch will also do well.

If you are not equipped to cut or split the timber yourself, you might have a sawmill custom-cut a piece for you. Have them cut the log into a pair of 4- or 5-inch thick tops and some 4 by 4s for the legs. Try to find a mill that is small enough that someone can get a message to the sawyer to break his routine, yet big enough that it is actually engaged in cutting wood.

You may get lucky. I was out at the mill a while back and spotted a stack of 4-inch-thick red maple timbers with paraffin wax on the ends. The brothers that run this mill wouldn't any more put wax on the ends of their timbers than they would tie pink ribbons on their cant hooks. I asked one of the brothers about this. He was more embarrassed than angry. Some boys from town had asked him to cut it for bench tops. He did, and they came out and carefully waxed the ends of the timbers to keep them from checking. The timbers had already begun to show signs of heavy warping, though, and they never came back to pick them up. This had been many months earlier, and the timbers had turned black and were on the verge of going bad. He offered them to me cheap and was glad to be rid of them.

I brought them home, where the wax on the ends provided a good hour's diversion for my four-year-old daughter, who found that it worked easily with my planes and chisels. It takes about two years for a timber of this thickness to dry enough to hold still, but in the meantime you can still get a lot of use out of it. Unless the tree was born to move, the minor distortions should be easily planed out as the wood settles down.

BUILDING UP A TOP

If you don't want to deal with a single heavy timber, you must build up the top from smaller pieces. Use pieces of dried 2 by 4 hardwood and glue enough of them together, broad face to broad face, to give you the width you want. You can reinforce the final assemblage with long bolts of threaded rod. This makes a very stable top, and the process of building it up gives you opportunities to bury bolts or nuts within the top to help anchor vises. The top for my paneled bench is built up of 2 by 4 pieces joined with splines and glue. Lacking enough wood to do otherwise, I

My Bench

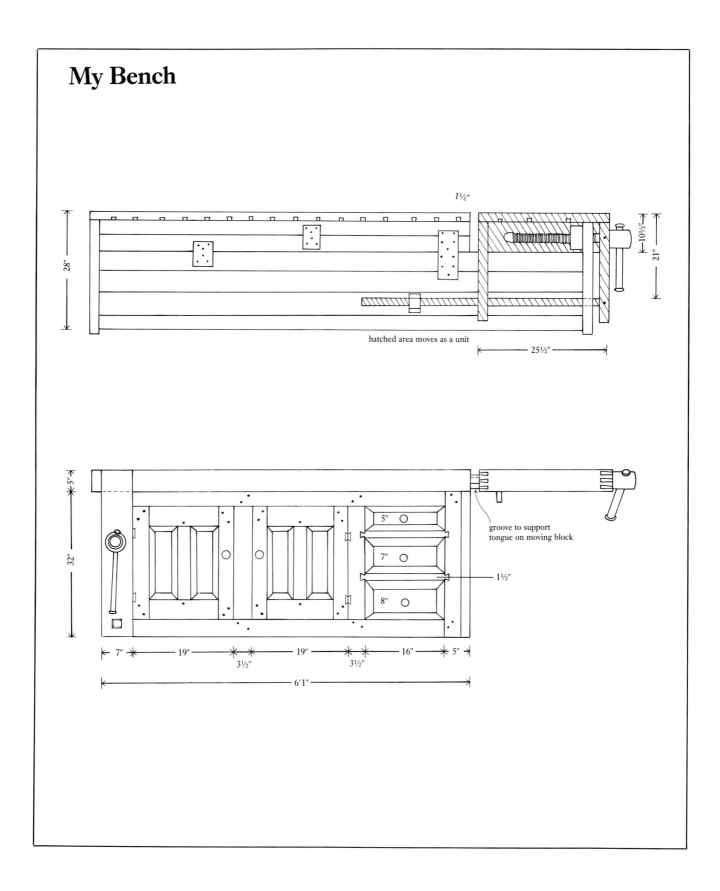

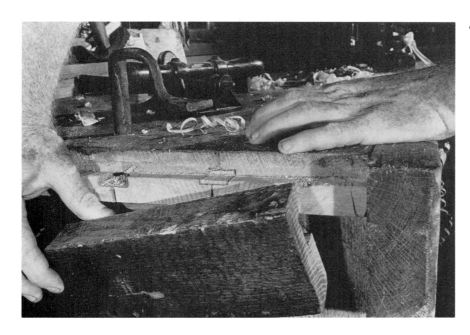

Splined joints in my old bench top.

joined them narrow face to narrow face and, consequently, it is only 2 inches thick. As it is well supported by the frame that it sits on, it doesn't flex.

LEGS

The simplest benches (and often the best) have legs simply morticed into the top. Not content with simple solutions, Roubo often showed a peculiar tenon and dovetail arrangement. The advantage of this joint is hard to see. The dovetail does keep the face of the legs flush with the front of the bench. And it adds a larger bearing surface and some additional stiffness to the legs. He does say that when the bench gets old and the legs loose, the tops of the mortices can be enlarged and wedges driven in to retighten them. This relies on the strength of the mortice and tenon to resist racking of the rectangular form, rather than on the braced design of table legs. Like Roubo, Bergeron noted that the tenons on more sophisticated benches go only three-quarters of the way through the top; this is the case for the benches in the Dominy shop. Only on commoner benches do the tenons protrude into the work surface.

LEG JOINTS

The earliest benches stood on four independent legs with no connections between them. When the legs are linked with rails to brace them and to support shelves and holding devices, three joints are commonly

[left]
Leg joint, "à la Roubo."

[right]
Haunched tenon joining skirt rail to leg (cheap wood—expensive joint).

used. First is the basic mortice and tenon—usually a simple affair, with each joint offset so that they do not interfere with each other. If the bench has a thinner top needing support on its front edge, it may be provided with a skirt just under the top, as on a table. This means that both the end and the long side rails meet the corner posts at the same point. The two tenons meet inside the post and must be mitered on their ends to give each its maximum strength. Also, because the mortice is near the top end of the leg, strength can be retained by using a tenon with a diminished haunch. This will keep the end of the mortice closed but allow the tenon to prevent twisting across the full width of the board.

FASTENERS

Woodworking on the highest level solves its own problems with its own material. Joints that interlock timbers are superior to those that rely on fasteners such as nails. Yet economy has its virtues, and there are quickly

cut, simple joints employing nuts and bolts to make a take-apart bench. Here, a shallow mortice and tenon is held in place by a bolt that reaches through the joint and engages a nut set into a hole bored partially through the tenoned piece. If you make this joint, remember that since you will not have access to the nut in the wood, you must turn the bolt head to tighten the joint. (I mention this because I know a fellow who bought carriage bolts instead of common bolts. Carriage bolts have round, unslotted heads with partially squared shanks to keep them from turning in the wood. It was too late to return them, and so he went ahead and worried them tight with a pair of pliers, a chisel, and a hammer, working late into the night.)

Nut sunk in the rail for bolting legs.

DRAWBORING

The way people move about, you may well want to be able to take your bench apart. When you peg through the joints, leave the pegs protruding

Roubo's End Vise

I made my bench with an end vise that uses a framed out-rigger to keep it tight in the track. It is similar to the one described by Roubo, but uses a manufactured bench screw and nut.

The end vise detailed by Roubo in 1771 measures about 14 inches long and 3½ inches wide and is as thick as the bench. The six sides of the box enclosing the screw are joined with tongues and grooves, rabbets, and mortice and tenon joints reinforced with glued pegs or screws. The cover piece (B, fig. 7) must be fastened with screws alone to allow access to the internal mechanism.

The back piece (D) and the end piece (F) are designed to keep the sliding box tight against the bench. Piece F (shown end-grain-on in figure 6) has an 8-inch tail which hooks over a retaining bar (G, figs. 6 and 7) on the underside of the bench top. The back piece (D, fig. 7) is flanged to fit into a slot in the edge of the bench. This piece is also seen in figure 12. Figure 10 shows the side of the bench ready to receive the box, along with the retaining bar (G).

The head of the box (E) also has a special function. As shown in figure 8, it links the screw to the box so that it will open when the screw is backed off. Two keys of iron, copper, or very hard wood ride in a groove turned in the shank of the screw.

In figure 8 you can also see that the nut for the wooden screw is actually an iron case filled with a soft metal casting. This nut has a 6-inch tail which is bolted into a mortice in the side of the bench. In the side view, figure 7, the nut is shown with its two bolts. Figure 9 shows a top view of the nut and its tail. (The following chapter will show you how to make wooden nuts and screws for vises and other devices.)

The opening through the nut for the casting must be about ⅜ inch larger than the diameter of the screw. Flare the opening on both ends and drill holes in the four sides of the nut so that the casting will be held solidly. Take a length of screw similar to that which you will use and coat it with fine clay mixed with glue. This coating gives the screw clearance and keeps the heat of the casting from scorching it.

When the coating is dry, position the screw in the nut and mold clay around it to prevent the molten metal from leaking out. Now, pour in the casting material, which is composed of two parts lead with one part anti-mony. When the metal is cold, remove the screw and the nut is done. The iron catches (figs. 2 and 3) which hold the work are about ¾ inch square and about an inch longer than the thickness of the bench. A spring on their side holds them at the proper height. One hook may be set in any of the holes which are cut every 4 inches in a line 1½ inches back from the edge of the bench, lined up with the middle of the screw. These holes are cut at an opposing angle to those in the vise box, as you see in figure 6, so the hooks stay tight and the board doesn't come loose.

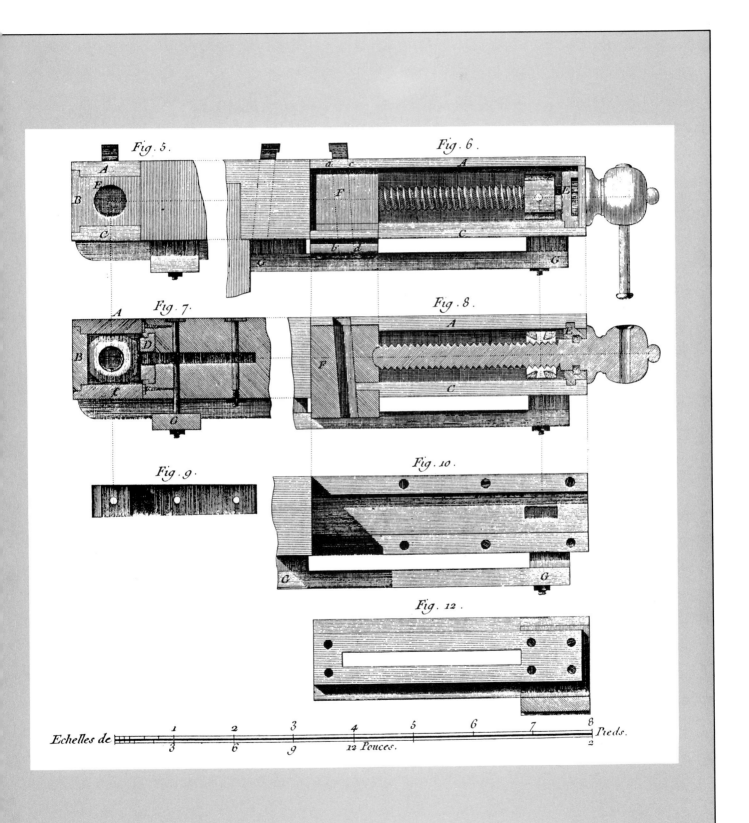

Fig. 5.

Fig. 6.

Fig. 7.

Fig. 8.

Fig. 9.

Fig. 10.

Fig. 12.

Echelles de ... 1 ... 2 ... 3 ... 4 ... 5 ... 6 ... 7 ... 8 Pieds.
3 ... 6 ... 9 ... 12 Pouces. ... 2

Scribe around the key to lay out the mortice for a tusk tenon.

on the hidden side so that you can drive them out when you want to. The pegs should be properly drawbored so that they pull the joint tight. To drawbore the joints, first bore the peg hole through the cheeks of the mortice without the tenon in place. Then put the tenon tight into the joint and, using either the lead screw of the auger used to bore the hole or a scratch awl, mark the location of the peg hole on it. Now pull the joint apart and bore the hole through the tenon, being sure to offset it about 1/8 inch *toward the shoulder* of the tenon.

When you reassemble the joint, you can either drive the tapered peg straight in or use a polished steel "draught-nayle" to make the initial compression. When you drive the peg, be sure that the underside of the morticed piece is well supported. I have seen beautiful work ruined because the offset of the hole caused the peg to miss the hole on the far side and split off the cheek.

TUSK TENON

Another pegging method is commonly used when the long rails pass through the horizontal bar between the legs of one end. The usual practice is to allow these tenons to pass through the end boards and hold them with a tapered key. This is the tusk tenon used in teutonic work. It is similar to the drawbored joint in that the tapered key pulls the joint tight. Be sure that the hole for the key extends back below the surface of the wood through which the tenon passes. Otherwise the peg will never be able to draw up the joint. (This is not done in Alabama, where the tusks-are-loosa.)

3

SCREWBOXES & TAPS

Many ingenious practizes in all trades, by a connexion and transferring of the observations of one Arte, to the use of another.

—Francis Bacon, 1605

WHETHER you want to clamp wood, press cider from apples, or adjust the drive tension of a spinning wheel, you need wooden screws and nuts. Two tools will enable you to reproduce as many screws and nuts as you need, all based (like life) on an initial ancestral helix. The first tool is the tap, which cuts the internal thread of the nut. The first threads that your tap must cut are those within the second tool, the die or "screwbox" itself, which is a wooden nut armed with a cutting iron.

Wooden screw making is strongly associated with the turner's trade. A screw is simply an inclined plane wrapped around a cylinder, and these cylinders need to be turned. The turner could also use his lathe to cut the threads into these cylinders, as well as the internal threads of nuts, but as you will find, the screwbox and tap are far more convenient.

THE LITTLE TAP

The tap for making internal threads up to about an inch in diameter is similar to those used when working in metal. It consists of a tapered steel spiral, fluted on four sides to create cutting teeth along its length. A wooden T-handle, which fits onto a tang at the top of the steel tap, allows you to twist it into the hole like an auger.

You could start with plain steel round stock equal to the outside diameter of the screw that you want to make and simply file out the tap—but if you have access to a forge, a little bit of smithing can save a lot of filing and grinding. Start with square stock that is slightly larger or round stock slightly smaller than the final diameter and forge it to a cruciform cross section between blacksmith's shaping tools called "fullers." Because I work alone, I use a fuller made from a piece of steel rod bent into a U shape. I sandwich the yellow hot blank for the tap into the U and strike the side of the rod with a hammer. Two hollows are formed at once. I then turn the stock and strike the other two faces. I taper the other end down into a tapered tongue for the tang. After forging, I file the business end as round as possible in preparation for laying out the threads.

You can make this tap from mild steel; the cutting is distributed between so many teeth that they will hold their edge for some time. Only about a 3-inch section needs to be threaded, so don't make too much work for yourself. It takes about six hours of forging and filing to make such a tap.

PERFECT PITCH

"Pitch" is the distance between the peaks of adjacent threads. A paper pattern will allow you to create your screw's spiral at the proper pitch and then transfer it to the screw. Cut out a rectangular piece of paper pre-

[opposite]
The hickory helix—George Wilson's cider press screw.

The tap and screwbox, with a wooden tap for bench screws in the background.

cisely equal in width to the desired circumference of the screw (and of the tap) and as long as the threaded section of the tap (3 inches is sufficient). Take a compass and pace off the width until you cross it in twelve equal steps. This twelfth of the circumference will be the pitch of the threads. Making the threads larger and farther apart would reduce your mechanical advantage, and making them smaller (less than one-eighteenth of the circumference) and closer would make them too weak.

With your compass thus set, start at the bottom corners of the rectangular paper and pace up the two sides. Now take a ruler and draw a line connecting the lower left corner with the first division up on the right. Continue making lines parallel to this first one, diagonally connecting the divider marks.

Wrap the paper around the tap to see that the lines join up as they should. If all is well, glue the paper around the tap. (If you have forged the flutes in the tap, the paper will have to bridge these gaps and maintain the form of a perfect cylinder.) When the glue is dry, take a triangular file and lightly cut precisely on the spiral line, working along the whole length of the tap. Clean off the paper and you will see the spiral lightly incised in the metal. File away the space between these lines with one

corner of a triangular file, forming a 60-degree valley. Let the peak be just to one side of the initial line. (The peaks should be the full diameter and not reduced by even the slight filing made through the paper.) Taper the end of the tap sufficiently to allow it to start in the hole in the wood. Refine the faces of the cutting edges so that they look sharp and you're ready to go.

File through the paper pattern into the forged tap blank.

TAPPING

Tapping takes a good bit of force. Inset the flat tang of the tap across, rather than along, the grain of the wooden handle to keep it from splitting. The hole to be tapped should be just a bit larger than the diameter of the tap at the bottom of its threads. This is the minor or root diameter of the screw. As you turn the tap into the hole, back it out occasionally to be sure that it does not jam with shavings. It may be wise to clamp the piece being tapped in a vise so that the internal pressure does not split it open along the grain.

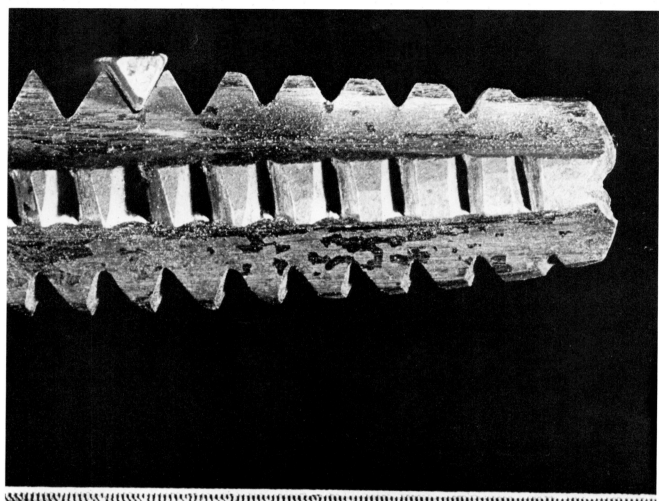

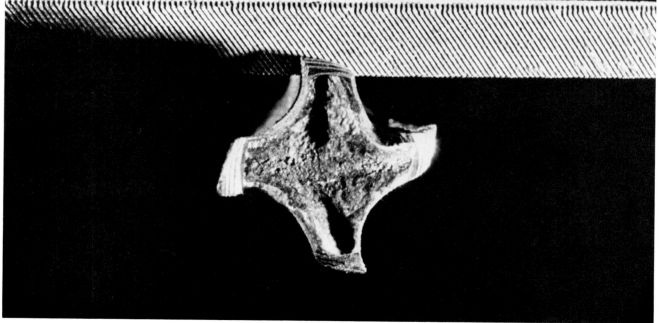

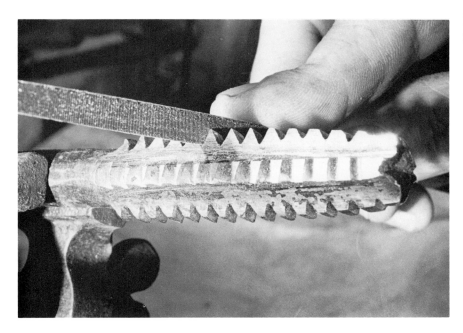

Taper the starting end of the tap to the root diameter.

THE DIE IS CAST

The screwbox takes about as long to make as the tap. Choose a block of very dry, hard wood, such as box, apple, pear, maple, dogwood, beech, or birch. The screwbox is made in two parts: the main body, which is threaded and equipped with the cutter, and the guide plate, which centers the blank wooden rod and feeds it into the cutter. The threaded block should be thick enough to accommodate about six turns of the thread. The guide plate needs to be only half as thick. The blocks should be made about twice as long as they are wide. If you wish to turn handles on either end of the thick block, its dimensions should be about 3 by 9 inches.

The holes in these two pieces, the large one through the guide plate and the threaded one in the big block, must be precisely concentric. Clamp the two pieces together and bore holes for quarter-inch-diameter alignment pins in diagonally opposing corners. Set in the pins (you could also use screws) and locate the center of the broad face of the two pieces. Inscribe the circumference of the hole in the guide plate (which should be just a hair larger than the diameter of the rod that you want to thread) with a compass, bore the small hole (the minor diameter) through both pieces, and then enlarge the one in the guide plate to the diameter inscribed by the compass. Alternatively, bore the large hole through the guide plate and stop just before you begin cutting into the main block. Now start the smaller auger in the same hole left by the lead screw of the larger one and continue the rest of the way through. Carefully cut the internal threads in the smaller hole with the tap and prepare to give it teeth.

[opposite]
Cutting your teeth. Two views of the filing.

[right]
Bore the root-diameter hole through the main block after boring the initial hole through the guide plate alone.

[below]
Tap through the main block.

THE V CUTTER

The V cutter is made from a square section of steel a little larger than the pitch distance of the threads you wish to cut. It must be made from tool steel that is capable of being hardened and tempered; I use scrap steel from old coil springs. This must be softened by heating it bright red hot and then allowing it to cool very slowly. After undergoing this process the steel can be shaped with files and hacksaws. The V should of course have the same 60-degree angle as the tap, exactly that of the slim taper files for saw sharpening. The cutting edge of the V should not be perpendicular to its length, but must be inclined forward about 10 degrees. This inclination ensures that the surface of the excavation in the wood is cut before the interior, which is a great way to keep the wood from breaking.

The cutter must be very sharp so that it will slice through the wood and not jam and start breaking off the threads. You can buy triangular slip stones to hone the inside of the V or you can grind the corner of a stone that you already have. It does not matter if the triangular file leaves the inside of the valley of the V slightly rounded. Just be sure that the outside is correspondingly shaped to meet it in a sharp edge. There must be no blunt spots.

The cutter will need to be hardened and tempered. Harden the cutter by heating it to a red glow and then cooling it quickly in an oil bath. Test the face of the cutter with the corner of a file to see if you can "pick" at the steel. If the cutter is hard enough, the file should skate off it like glass. If it is still too soft, try quenching it again at red-yellow heat. To temper it so that it will not be so hard that it shatters, heat the end away from the cutting edge until you see colors move down the metal. When

Shape the V cutter with a slim taper file.

the straw color reaches the cutting edge and just begins to turn to peacock, quench it to halt the softening at this point.

If you have not done this before, you would do well to take it to a blacksmith and have her do it for you. Watch how it's done, and you will know next time.

POSITIONING THE CUTTER

You must position the cutter exactly right in the screwbox. Separate the two blocks of the screwbox. Using a square, scratch a line on the joining face of the thicker piece that is perpendicular to the long side of the block and passes through the precise center of the threaded hole. Set the cutter on the block so that it is perpendicular to this line with the point of the V protruding very slightly into the hole beyond the peaks of the threads. The V cutter must be inset into the wood at this point so that its cutting edge begins the spiral of the internal thread. (You may want to try the other side of the hole, diagonally opposite, if it looks as though you might make a better fit there.) With a needle, scratch around the cutter to mark where it must go in.

As you chisel away the space for the cutter, cut the end of the space opposite the cutting edge deeper so that the cutter will be sitting at the same angle as the inclination of the threads. It's all much easier to do than to explain. Keep trying the cutter in place to see that it looks as if it will do what it is supposed to.

The cutter must be held very firmly in position with no room to move about. You may need to shim it with strips of tin to align it in its final

Chisel the seat for the cutter just ahead of the start of the thread.

*Screws are the simplest means to lock **the** cutter in place.*

position. Lock it into place with three screws or an L-shaped bolt that hooks over it. The bolt is more secure because it passes through the block and is held by a nut rather than screw threads in the wood.

At this point you can cut an escape for the shavings leading from the cutter to the outside. This should be as deep as the cutter seat and include the back of the V slot in the cutter.

THREADING SCREWS

Turn your screw shaft from air dried stock (not too dry): elm, hickory, Osage orange, apple, or similar stuff. Narrow it slightly at one end to help it feed into the screwbox. See that the surface is smooth and unflawed. Small pieces can be held in one hand while the screwbox is held in the other and the two pieces twisted like a pepper mill. Bigger pieces need to be held in a vise. Soap, wax, or oil will help keep things moving smoothly.

The guide plate needs to be removable so that, when necessary, you can "bull nose" the screwbox right up to a shoulder on the screw, such as you would find on a screw for a clamp. In such cases, work as before until you reach the shoulder, back off the screwbox, remove the guide plate, crank back to your starting place and then cut right up to the end.

THE BIG TAP

For nuts much over an inch in diameter, the steel tap is not as practical. Screws for bench vises run from about 2 to 3 inches in diameter—which would call for one big mean tap indeed. Fortunately, the tap used to make these large nuts is easy to make. It is composed of two principal pieces: a single cutter-equipped cylinder incised with a sawn screw thread and a special nut made to fit this spiral kerf. It works by using the special nut to pull the cylinder and its scraper-cutter, spiraling through the inside of the hole. By making several passes, setting the cutter to take a little deeper bite each time, the internal threads may be cut to their full depth. This tap can be used for screw diameters ranging from about 1½ inches for large clamps to 16 inches for making paper presses.

MAKING IT

Select a piece of dry hickory or other tough, hard wood and turn it to a perfect cylinder equal to the diameter of the hole that you want to tap. Its length should be about four times the depth of the thickest nut you might want to tap. A suitable portion of one end should be left large enough to be bored to take a handle. At the opposite end, maintain the accurate diameter right to the very edge and then cut off sharp and square.

LAYING OUT

Rather than use the previous paper pitch plan, you can also lay out a very large screw directly on the wooden cylinder. Draw lengthwise lines down the cylinder that divide it into six or eight equal parts around its circumference. The more divisions you make, the more accurate the thread will be. Determine the pitch for the screw diameter (one-twelfth of the circumference) and then divide this into as many parts as you have made parallel lines on the cylinder.

Start at the end of one of the lines and mark it clearly as the beginning. Draw a line with a pencil and a flexible ruler from this zero point to one compass-step up on the first line to the right, on to two compass-steps up on the second line to the right, and so on around until you again cross the starting line, a full pitch distance from the start. Continue right to the end, following whole thread widths paced off from this initial helix. Stop the spiral when you are as far from the shoulder of the head as the thickness of the thickest nut you might want to tap, and then some. (I hate to mention this, but the half-inch-wide "tractor bars" that you pull off of computer paper will also give you the perfect pitch for a 2-inch-diameter screw. Wrap it around the cylinder like a tight candy-cane and cut on the spiraling junction.)

You now need to saw along this helical line to a consistent depth. A staircase saw that exposes a measured depth of saw blade is ideal for this. You can also make such a saw by riveting or screwing a slotted wooden handle on a narrow blade so that only a fraction is exposed. You can also fold a butt hinge flat, put a bolt and wingnut through its screw holes and clamp it on a hacksaw blade. Either way, carefully saw the spiral from one end to the other.

At the far end of the sawn thread, bore and chisel a square mortice that will allow you to position a V scraper so that its cutting edge is precisely on the diameter of the cylinder. The cutter must be canted so that it sits square to the thread rather than parallel to the axis of the

Saw the spiral in the big tap.

Inset *the scraper in a mortice passing* **through** *the threaded shaft, locking it* **with** *a long, finely tapered wedge.*

Tapering shims support the sheet-metal collars that engage the spiral saw kerf.

cylinder. The width of the cutter (and the mortice it sits in) is equal to the width of the pitch. Grind this cutter from an old flat file so that its point makes a 60 degree angle. A gently tapering wooden wedge holds the cutter in place. Both the cutter and the wedge should be just the right length to allow them to fit within the diameter of the cylinder. Make a small hollow in the cylinder ahead of the cutter to collect and hold the scrapings as the cutter advances.

THE NUT

The special nut to engage the saw kerf is also easy to make. Take an inch-thick board and bore a hole through its center equal to the diameter of the tap cylinder. Find a piece of sheet steel of the same gauge as the thickness of the spiral saw kerf. Saw and file it into two rectangular pieces with semi-circular cutouts that will fit into the sawn spiral on the cylinder. Fit the cylinder through the bored board and set the two metal pieces into opposite sides of the spiral kerf. Using these prepositioned plates as a guide, make two similarly shaped slanting wooden supports to fit under the plates. Fasten the finished pieces together with screws.

On the opposite face of the board, fasten two spacer blocks that are half again as thick as the cutter in the tap. These will give the cutter a place to go when it reaches the far side of the nut being tapped. It is a good idea to arm the faces of these spacers with screws or nails with their heads cut off and sharpened into spikes. This will keep the nut from slipping, for, as you will see, there is quite a bit of torque involved in tapping a big nut.

Set the scraper to cut deeper on each pass.

TAPPING WITH THE BIG TAP

You will be very pleased with how well this tap works. Bore a hole the same size as the cylinder through the piece that you want to tap. Set the cylinder through the hole and screw its nut up tight to the victim. Check the centering of the nut and clamp it tight to the piece to be tapped. With a hammer and a punch, set the cutter so that it protrudes slightly. Be sure that the wedge is tight and start turning the handle to advance the cutter clockwise through the wood. If it seems to be too hard to turn, back off the cutter a bit and try again. When you break through on the far side, see that all the scrapings fall free, back out counter-clockwise, and knock the cutter out a bit further to take a deeper bite. Run the cutter through, setting it deeper and deeper, as many times as it takes to reach the proper depth of thread in the nut. If you have made the screw first, try it in the nut to see how it runs. It's much easier to make another pass to cut the nut larger than to try to put wood back in to make it smaller.

GIANT SCREWS

The screwbox works well for screws up to about 3 inches in diameter. For screws between 1¾ and 3 inches in diameter you will need to make a screwbox with two cutters, the first making a shallow cut and the second the full-depth cut. Aligning these two cutters in the screwbox is a "matter of great nicety." Beyond 3 inches, say for cider or printing presses, you will be obliged to cut the threads by hand.

Make the cylinder for these big screws as accurately as you can from a

[right]
*To tap a thick workbench top for a vise,
first bore the hole, then chisel an opening
on the underside to allow you to insert
the collar that engages the spiral on the
tap.*

[below]
*A sophisticated tap for making workbench
screws (collection of Colonial
Williamsburg).*

[opposite above]
*Chopping a cider press screw, from
Bergeron's* Manuel du Tourneur, *
1816.*

[opposite below]
*The cider press. As in many large screws,
these threads are blunter, about 80
degrees.*

solid piece of elm or apple. If you cannot get to a lathe large enough to turn your cylinder, do your best by starting with a square cross-section, then making it eight sided, then sixteen sided, and so on. Lay out the pitch around the cylinder as before, but this time, mark two helices. With a pencil of another color, mark a second line running exactly down the middle of the thread. Take your saw and cut in on this second line for the full depth of the screw. (Remember that this depth is less than the distance between threads. Draw an equilateral triangle and you will see what I mean.) When you finish sawing, take a very sharp chisel and gradually enlarge this long kerf into a V that touches the first line on either side. Clean up your chisel work with a fine rasp. Make the matching internal threads with the big tap described earlier and invite your friends over to see the world's largest hickory nut.

4 LATHES

Through the door came the regular hum of a lathe.
The princess timidly opened the door which moved
noiselessly and easily. She paused at the entrance.
The prince was working at the lathe and after glancing
round continued his work.

—Tolstoy, *War and Peace,* 1865

A bow-spring lathe with roller reduction.

I can easily understand why Tolstoy's prince took solace in wood turning. The spinning wheels have the same hypnotic effect as a running stream or the rolling flames of a fire. Even the rankest novice is rewarded with perfection, the most indolent dissipation wearing the guise of productivity. Like the game of chess, the skills of turning can be quickly learned but the depth of its challenge can take a lifetime to plumb. The equipment can range from a few sticks and a string to remarkably involved (and expensive) machines to satisfy the most jaded hardware nut.

There is no eccentricity in aristocratic wood turning either. Turning was one of the few manual skills that a gentleman could indulge in. One of the earliest books on lathe work, Frenchman Charles Plumier's 1749 *Art of Turning*, is written for an elite audience. The author stated that he never "looked upon the lathe as anything but an honorable occupation for passing some pleasurable hours," thus assuring the reader that although he might work, he would never sweat.

Lathes are supposed to save time, but in one shop where I worked the foreman insisted on jobbing out all the wood turning. He would not allow a lathe in the shop because he feared that we "would spend more time wood turning than working."

The earliest lathes used reciprocating motion; pulling a cord wrapped around the stock sets it spinning first one way and then the other. The stock alternately makes four or five revolutions in each direction. You cut only when the wood is spinning towards you from the top. Originally, an assistant pulling the cord provided the power. In later versions, the turner worked alone, pulling the cord with a foot treadle; the return stroke was provided by a spring pole attached to the other end. These lathes are simple, direct and powerful. Those who deride such lathes as being only "fifty percent efficient" are blind to joy and lead a barren existence.

The other form of turner-powered lathe is the treadle-flywheel lathe. Leonardo da Vinci is credited with the invention of this machine in around 1500, as the earliest drawing of one appears in his sketchbook. The reciprocal motion of foot power is converted to full circular motion by a crankshaft and the speed increased and power stored by the flywheel-drive pulley. When properly constructed, treadle lathes are reliable, fast, and a great source of pleasure.

You might wish to start with a simple yet sturdily built spring-pole lathe. This can later form the foundation for conversion to a flywheel-treadle lathe, should you be so moved.

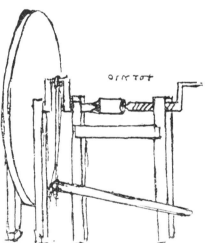

[above]
The spring-pole lathe of the early Middle Ages.

[below]
Leonardo's revolutionary flywheel treadle lathe.

A POLE LATHE FRAME

My spring-pole lathe frame is made from heavy yellow pine. All the parts are roughly 4 by 6s. The critical parts are the bed rails, which hold the moveable "puppets." Their actual measurements are not important, so

Dovetailed rails in a pine lathe frame. The tool rest is supported by sliding blocks morticed through the puppets.

long as they are parallel. If they are not, ease of adjustment for differing lengths of stock will suffer. The bed rails dovetail into the sides of the uprights, and the uprights straddle the bottom crosspiece in a common bridle joint. It can be taken apart easily, yet is quite sturdy. If carefully cut and not taken apart too often, the joints will not need to be pegged.

The dovetails joining bed to upright are simple to cut, but I have noticed that they are baffling to workers who are used to thinking in terms of machine technique. To cut the rail end of the joint, all you need to do is lay it out with a gauge and ruler, then saw what you can and chisel away the rest. When the rails are done, place them on the uprights, scribe around their outlines, and saw and chisel their space.

A versatile tool rest on a spring-pole lathe at Old Salem, North Carolina.

The puppets that support the pikes and the tool rest are mirror images, right and left handed. They hold the conical iron pikes on which the wood spins and the brackets to support the tool rest. Each has a tail that locks it into place on the rails. This tail extends below the bottom of the rails, where it is pierced by a mortice that extends higher than the underside of the rails. When you drive a tapered wedge through this mortice, it quickly locks the puppet tight in place. The action is similar to that of a draw-bore pin or the tusk tenon used in bench construction.

The lathe is as simple to use as it is to construct. Mount a long, springy dry pole overhead so that the tip end is over the work space in the lathe. Roughly round the stock with a drawknife and center it between the beeswaxed pikes. Tie a cord to the end of the pole and wrap it around the stock so that it passes on the side facing you. Tie the free end of the cord to a 3-foot stick to use for a treadle on the floor. Cut on the downstroke, rest on the upstroke, and turn, turn, turn again.

BOW SPRINGS

I had not used a spring-pole lathe for too many years before the problem developed—a painfully callused area on the top of my head. This is not a new problem; in 1775 a Monsieur Hulot of Paris (one of Roubo's neighbors) wrote that "when you do your turning in a low-ceilinged room, you run the risk of hitting yourself on the head with the spring-pole each time you put your foot down." Rather than slowly pound themselves through the floor, he noted, clever woodturners replaced the spring pole with a "bow of wood or steel."

Like an archer's bow, a bow intended for a lathe spring needs strength and resilience. If anything, life on a lathe is even more demanding. A few minutes of turning can equal a year's shooting in Sherwood Forest. A strong spring helps to lift your foot so that you can punch down again quickly. A weak, slow bow is much more tiring to work with.

I have used black locust, hickory, and Osage orange for bows, and the last of the three came out the best. Osage orange is one of the classic native American bow woods, as evidenced by its other common name, "bois d'arc" or the Americanized "bodark." This first cousin to the mulberry (the green, grapefruit-sized aggregate fruits look like mulberries on steroids) is native to the Mississippi Valley, but has become widespread as an ornamental. Osage bows are interesting to make because you shape them by absolutely going with the flow of the grain. The light-colored sapwood remains down the back of the bow, its undulations forming the baseline of the final dimensions.

Other woods may be worked in the same manner, but with less attention to the grain. Split a 5-foot-long section of tree about 5 inches in diameter into eight pieces. Choose the best of the eight and carefully shave off the bark. Shave down the sides of the grain until it is 1 inch wide down its length. If the wood is reasonably dry, you can continue; if not, get the third-best piece from the tree and work on it so you will have something to use while the good piece dries. Measure to find and mark the mid-length; then measure out to each end marking 6-inch intervals. Leaving the middle foot 1 inch thick, reduce the thickness by ⅛ inch every 6 inches until you reach the ends. Make the bow 1½ inches wide in the middle foot and taper it similarly to the ends. This is enough to start with. The proper bending can be achieved only by tillering, that is, drawing the bow and shaving it until it is right.

Eighteenth-century leaf-spring lathe.

LEAF SPRINGS

You could take the bow that you just made off of the lathe and play Robin Hood with it. A lathe bow doesn't have to be this way. M. Hulot stated his preference for a bow comprising a stack of three thin slats of fir. The three slats are split radially from the billet, 3 inches wide and ¼ inch thick. The longest one (placed on the top of the stack) runs 3½ feet; each slat is slightly shorter toward the bottom of the stack, like a set of common leaf springs. They are held by an iron collar in the middle and iron caps on the ends. It is smaller and springier than an archer's bow, but it won't shoot an arrow.

DOWNSHIFTING

There is a problem with using bows on lathes, though. They are very strong but have little travel. The spring pole works well because it gives an even pull over a long run. Short bows are either too stiff or too weak. The way around this is to employ a simple device that trades distance for strength: the pulley. By running the drive cord over a pulley mounted at the pull point on the bow string, the draw weight is cut in half and the travel of the cord doubled.

This is usually enough for ordinary wooden bows, but extra-stiff bows need the additional downshifting of a cord-mounted roller. Here, the bow string is tripled, the three strings passing through the roller close to its perimeter. When a cord is wrapped around the roller and then pulled, the roller turns and the strings are twisted like the tension cord of a bow saw. The twisting shortens the strings, and they bend the bow. A lot of cord pulling gives a little bow bending.

MOUNTING

The great advantage of the bow spring is that it can be mounted directly onto the lathe frame. The lathe is thus able to be moved about when necessary. You can easily pick the whole thing up and work outside in good weather, or work by the fire when it is cold. For my own lathe, I found a limb of tulip poplar that had just the right arch to position the bow over the work. I fastened this piece to the lathe by simply notching it to fit around the back of the bed. Even without a wedge it stays in place and can be moved or removed when needed. I must say it is an odd looking thing when put together. It has the organically lurid look of the cover of some never-written Edgar Rice Burroughs novel, "Spindal, Woodturner of Mars." It is one of the few things that I have made which caused me to break into laughter when I stepped back to look at it.

One of the characteristics of a lathe driven by a cord wrapped around the workpiece is that the cord is eventually going to be in the way. For this

Pulling the cord turns the roller, twists the rope, and bends the bow.

reason, I prefer a loose foot treadle to one that is hinged to the floor because the cord can be repositioned by just moving your foot to one side as you work. The bow or spring pole can also be easily slid over to move the cord to another place. In his laminated bow lathe mentioned earlier, Hulot takes this a step further by mounting his bow on rollers which slide along a track mounted over the lathe bed. Quite a rig.

LEVERED LATHES

The stiffness of the bow spring can be dealt with by a pulley or roller, but a short strong spring pole calls for taking another tack: the lever. The next lathe from M. Hulot's book is clearly designed for amateurs. It is apparently the author's invention, rather than a common item of the time. Still, the design is so clever that many a one must have been turning in Paris in those years before a larger revolution came down.

A Portable, Folding Lathe

HULOT, 1775

Devotees of wood turning are sometimes poorly situated to have a permanently mounted lathe, or they may have only a small apartment to work in. For them, I have designed a lathe that may be folded up and stored in a corner.

The two wooden bed-beams are 3 to 4 inches square, and connected together by two tie-beams, G and H. Two of the legs, D and F, are permanently connected to the front bed-beam with mortice and tenon joints. The two others, C and E, are joined with double tenons to the long cross beam M, N, which is about 9 inches wide. These legs are attached with hinges on the under side as seen in O, fig. 6. The wooden brace I, K, is moveable at I, pivoting about an iron screw. The other end, K, is notched to catch on a similar iron screw; holding the legs at their proper spacing. When it is unhooked and folded along side of leg C, the leg may hinge at O, to fold up against leg D. The other end folds at the same time so that the lathe can be stored in a space no more than a foot deep.

The shelf L, with its little rim around three sides, attaches to the bed-beam, A, with little iron hinges. When you have removed the rocking arm pillar and the two puppets, it will flip over to cover the two bed-beams. This shelf gives you a place to keep tools and work in progress.

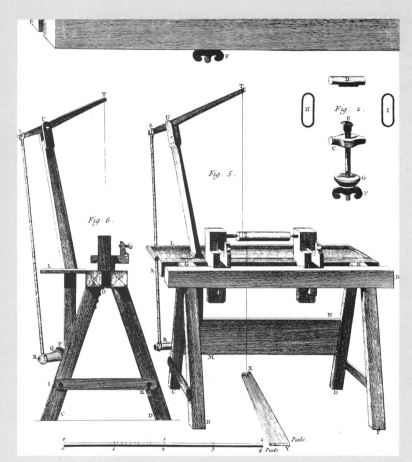

MY TREADLE LATHE

The year was 1970, and I was sure that a treadle lathe was the answer. I remember standing under the aspens in front of the communal kitchen high in the Rockies, expounding on treadle lathe economics. I thought that if we had a treadle lathe, we would be able to make spinning wheels to sell and we wouldn't have to eat soyburgers every day. None of us had ever seen a real treadle lathe, however, and with nowhere to begin, we didn't.

Margaret's ancient diesel Mercedes carried us east one winter to see our families. Along the way we stopped in Colonial Williamsburg, and in the cabinetmaker's shop was a treadle lathe. I took a photograph, but it was two years later that I finally built a copy of the lathe from this picture. By that time I was living in North Carolina again and made the lathe to use in a film on the history of furniture making. Later, I used it to make woodenware at craft fairs. Competition was pretty tough at the time, so I turned to showmanship. My gimmick was to turn spoons on the lathe with one hand and foot—while hewing a dough bowl with the other hand—while playing a harmonica. Frankly, I needed the business and had to swallow my pride—as I almost did the harmonica.

I have used this lathe for more than a decade. Many people have seen it and wanted to make one like it but did not want to proceed without a set of plans. Since I never had plans to begin with, I couldn't provide any. It is the sort of thing easily made by people who don't know any better, but agonized over by the sophisticated.

FRAME

At the time the only predimensioned stock that I had was Douglas fir. The lathe is thus very light and tends to creep about. It is great, though, when I have to take it on the road. The bed consists of three right triangles connected by four horizontal bars, the top two of which form the bed rails of the lathe. The vertical members of the two triangles on the left are built up from 2 by 6s; the extra width is necessary to house the headstock and idler pulleys.

HEADSTOCK

I got the bearings for my lathe from a scrapyard and from a dealer in motor bearings. Try to find sealed bearings that will better endure the dust and dirt. You must have at least one thrust bearing for the headstock pulley that runs the drive center, as it will receive considerable pressure while pinching the stuff being turned. The axle must have a thrust collar mounted on it to run against this thrust bearing. This collar can also serve to connect the pulley to the axle. Before you bore the axle hole

The treadle lathe at Williamsburg, now in the Geddy Foundry.

through the hardwood pulley, bore a shallow hole just large enough to set this collar into, then bore the smaller axle hole all the way through. The pulley will wobble a bit if the axle is not precisely centered, but you can turn it true once it is in place and being driven by the flywheel.

Perhaps your shop already has enough idlers in it, but your lathe will need yet another to help keep your belt tight. The idler on my lathe is

My treadle lathe.

simply another bearing-mounted roller on the back side of the headstock pulley. It serves to increase the surface contact of the drive cord on the working pulley and prevents slipping. My idler, however, is not adjustable and therefore little help when the drive cord starts stretching. The Williamsburg lathe does have an adjustable idler, and this is an improvement I recommend.

The headstock with drive and idler pulleys mounted on their bearings.

FLYWHEEL

I also built the flywheel from standard stock. The spokes are 2 by 4s half lapped in their middles. The rim of the flywheel is cut from four segments of 2 by 8. I made the mistake of sawing away the segments so that they took the form of a wagon wheel. Considering that you want the flywheel to be as heavy as possible, it would be smarter to round these pieces on the outside only. The segments are held together, and to the spokes, by nailing on two outer rings of ¾-inch stock. Cut these outer rings so that their joints are staggered with those of the inner ring.

The connection between the axle and the flywheel is crucial. It must be able to transmit all the force from the foot treadle to the flywheel. I used iron plumbing flanges and hex head bushings to make the connection. The hex head bushings are necessary to reduce the flange bore to an actual ½ inch so that the crankshaft (a ½-inch bolt bent to shape) will fit snug. (Although the iron flange will be marked "½," this refers to the inside diameter of the pipe that threads into it.) Once the wheel is positioned properly, you will need to drill an ⅛-inch hole through flange, bushing, and axle to insert a pin to lock it all up.

In order for the flywheel to turn true, its axle must be perfectly centered. Don't be concerned with balance yet; just see that you don't have any wobble or eccentricity (at least not on your lathe). Set together the connecting flanges, the flywheel, the crankshaft, and the bearings that it will run on. Center the flanges on the flywheel as well as you can with just one wood screw fastening each flange to the wheel. Knock together some means to suspend the wheel on its bearings and give the

The idler tension adjustment on the Williamsburg lathe. One of the adjusting wingnuts is hidden in this view.

wheel a spin. Set an indicator near the rim of the wheel and note any deviations. Reset the flanges until it runs right.

I have never had any luck with flat drive belts. Apparently, I have been using the wrong kind of leather—poor quality stuff that stretches and slips. All of my successful ventures have been with round leather belting, the kind used in driving treadle sewing machines. This is available from people who supply shoe repair equipment. Both the flywheel and the pulley must be grooved for this belting to run in; this is easily done with a V-shaped scraping tool or even the corner of a chisel as the wheel and pulley are spun by hand.

The Treadle Lathe

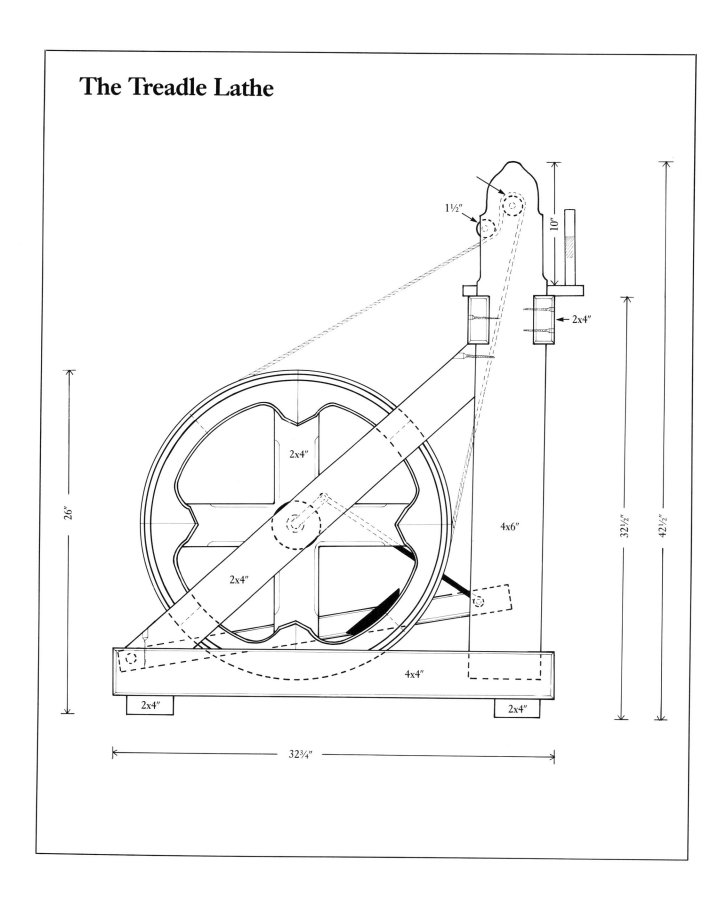

The Treadle Lathe

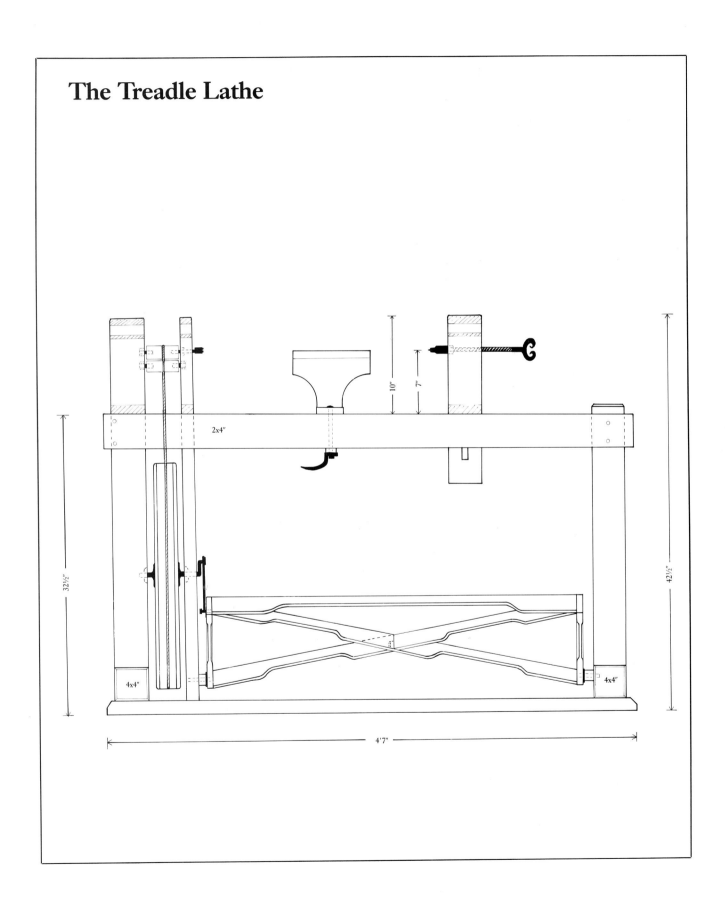

It would be better to make your flywheel solid and heavy.

TREADLE

The treadle should be as light and rigid as possible. The design that I use is nailed together from 1 by 3s, but cantilevered in such a way that the end away from the rod connecting to the flywheel is quite stiff. The back end pivots on lagbolts protected by washers.

The connecting rod attaches to a bolt set 2 feet away from the pivot point of the treadle. The point at which you link the connecting rod to the treadle determines the vertical travel of your foot when you are turning. This is a matter of leverage, bearing directly on the question of power versus the speed of the lathe. Try different arrangements as you see fit. I used quarter-inch-diameter iron for the connecting rod, but wood or even leather (it only pulls) will do.

When the treadle is connected to the flywheel by the connecting rod, it becomes a part of the wheel, an extra weight at one point on the perimeter. It seems to me that this extra weight should be counterbalanced on the wheel so that all is even again. I used a five-pound lead weight on the

wheel in this manner and it works. Experts, however, say that the wheel should be left alone and the back end of the treadle counterweighted if necessary. I haven't settled this question in my mind. Perhaps the best thing would be to experiment and see if there is less vibration. The influence of the weight of the treadle on the wheel is further complicated by the presence of the turner's foot on the treadle. It is a quandary to me.

I mounted the flywheel on the crankshaft with an assemblage of plumbing fixtures.

TAIL STOCK AND TOOL REST

With the exception of the adjusting screw, the tail stock is identical to the one that I use on spring-pole lathes. I would use the screw adjustment more often if it were a bit stouter. It tends to flex at full extension, and so I use it only when I need extra clearance, such as in hollowing work. I inset the nut for the threaded rod into the wood of the tailstock and covered it with a brass plate. By offsetting the hole in the plate from that in the nut, I hoped to make the adjustment tight enough to hold at any

Wedges and screws hold tail stock and tool rest.

point. It would be better, though, to rely on a setscrew. In any design, keep a candle or a bit of grease handy to lubricate the pike of the tail stock. It makes a big difference.

Some turners seem to derive as much enjoyment from arguing over tool rest positions and sharpening angles for their gouges as they do from the actual turning. I work with a tool rest that is just below the rotational axis of the work. The wedge and mortice arrangement that locks the tail stock in position would work just as well on the tool rest, except that the tool rest must be adjusted more often, and it gets to be a nuisance. I used a bolt and levered nut to make this a little faster and more convenient.

Your treadle lathe should serve you well. If you have not already been seduced by wood turning, you will soon discover its delights. As Plumier wrote in 1749, "There are hardly any people of dignity who do not attempt to excell in this art."

5 TOOL CHESTS

*. . . and it was after long searching that I found
the carpenter's chest, which was indeed a very useful
prize to me, and much more valuable than a ship
loading of gold.*

—Daniel Defoe, *Robinson Crusoe*, 1719

MY newfound prize sat behind me as I rolled down the dark, rainy road back to the shop. It had been won from the city rather than from a shipwreck, but my excitement nearly equaled that of the marooned mariner when he rafted his tool chest–treasure back to the island. The distraction of the mysteries within arm's reach caused me to run off the road once as I rummaged blindly, pulling out a brace, a gauge, a plane.

The letter that had led me to the tool chest had borne a four-month-old postmark when I saw it. Some folks had just moved into an old house, in back of which was a garden shed full of junk. Among this junk was an old tool chest which they didn't want and decided to sell. They were in a city right far off, but they had heard that I was interested in this sort of thing and asked me to come look at it. I figured it was worth the gamble.

I found them in their back yard, sitting in lawn chairs around a large dirty box. From the fuzzy-felt texture of the worn places I could see right away that the box was made from tulip poplar. That meant it was American, rather than English, perhaps even southern. It looked good.

The lid of the chest was off its hinges and lying propped against the back. It had been scrawled over with blue carpenter's chalk in a child's hand. The mortice lock was missing and had been replaced by a stamped metal hasp and a rusty cheap combination lock. The folks had set out a few of the tools, but most just lay piled in the filth of the chest. Half of the

Inside the chest. The rack of moulding planes is concealed beneath the sliding tray.

contents of the chest was trash: lengths of iron water pipe, cracked electrical fixtures, and auto parts with peeling chrome. The tools within told a sad tale.

In the top tray was a 2-inch-wide paring chisel, its pear-shaped box-wood handle mushroomed and split into three pieces, its edge chipped and blunted. They were good tools, bearing hardly any sign of use—but much of abuse. Some were in mint condition, except those that had been smashed by a hammer. Someone—afternoon vandals, rock-chopping children—had broken into the chest and and trashed it.

Price was the immediate question. How much was this lot worth to me? I don't like to buy and sell tools as some folks do, but I see a lot of catalogs and occasionally go to auctions, and so I had an idea of the going rate for each of the items in the chest. I began to pick through them, list them, and assign a "fair" price to each of them. One after the other I studied, pondered, and wrote down a price. Eventually my list looked like this:

Boring machine w/2 bits	$ 60.00
Moulding planes—9	90.00
Bench planes—6	90.00
Gouges—11	45.00
Broad axe	15.00
Adz	15.00
Gauges—2	15.00
Clapboard gauge—1	5.00
Panel cutter—2	15.00
Brace—1	50.00
Plow plane w/irons	50.00
Whetstone	5.00
Bevel	5.00
Drawknife	2.00
Saw	5.00
Chest	100.00
Total	$567.00

Five hundred and sixty-seven dollars is a lot of money, but I had priced everything at the level at which I would not hesitate to buy. I was trying to walk that thin line between coming across as a cheapskate or a fool. In spite of my upbringing, I went for the fool and rounded up to the nearest hundred.

"I've totalled them up," I said. "Looks to me like about five-fifty, but I think six hundred is closer to it."

There was the faintest flattening in my host's smile. "Well," he said, "I guess that would be all right."

Shrewd bargainer that I am, I couldn't let it rest there. "How about six-fifty?"

Back on the road through the rainstorm a wave of "buyer's remorse" shook me with a cold chill. Idiot! I suddenly thought. I'd been taken!

The Old Chest

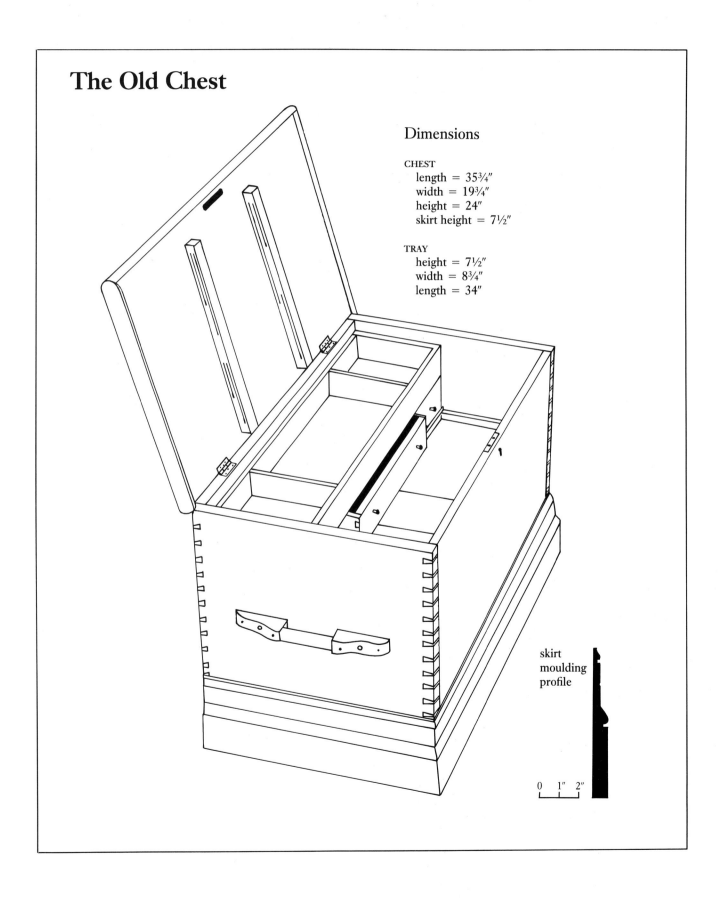

Dimensions

CHEST
length = 35¾″
width = 19¾″
height = 24″
skirt height = 7½″

TRAY
height = 7½″
width = 8¾″
length = 34″

skirt
moulding
profile

0   1″   2″

The square-ended screws usually date from before 1850. The cast-iron butt hinge is also typical of this period.

Whoever heard of buying a boring machine, a slick, a broadaxe, a carpenter's adze, and a chest of joiner's tools all in the same go? Someone had put all this together just to trick me!

But the more I thought about it, the more ridiculous that fear seemed. Besides, with tricks like that, who needed treats? No, it didn't look like a setup, but it certainly was a mystery. Perhaps I'd find the answer when I studied the chest more carefully.

It was too late to take the chest to the shop, so I went right home and began cleaning it out that night. The plumbing pipe and automotive trash went into a bag and the tools into neat rows on the floor. A piece of cardboard with faded purple ink was in one of the drawers. Even under ultraviolet light I could make out only the words "were made by hand." Late that night I finally made sense of it: "when windows were made by hand." At some point someone had displayed these tools in something like a family museum.

The first thing to examine on an old chest is the screws. After about 1850 wood screws were machine made with sharp points. Prior to that, the threads were either hand filed or die cut with a square point. The cast-iron hinges on the back of the chest were doubtless the original hardware, and sure enough the screws were the characteristic square-ended variety with offset V-bottomed slots. The chest was probably made before 1850. But what about the tools? I would need expert help to read their story. I returned the tools to their places so that before the shop opened the next morning I could take the chest to Jay Gaynor, Curator of Mechanical Arts at Colonial Williamsburg.

Ash, Wright, and Butcher—English manufacturers of the chisels, backsaw, and plane irons.

Jay looked at the dovetail saw first. The teeth were broken and cracked as though it had been used to cut through nails. The maker's stamp on the stiffening back read I WRIGHT   GERMAN STEEL. A quick check in one of his books showed that four I Wrights had manufactured saws in Sheffield, England, prior to 1850. During that period the mark "German Steel" was a common indication of high quality, the steel having been imported from Germany. Knight's *American Mechanical Dictionary* of 1876 defined German steel as being "made of charcoal-iron obtained from bog-iron or the sparry carbonate."

The brace, plated with inset brass, was unmarked and had less to say. The shrinking wood had caused the brass to pop free of its screws. Jay looked at the button on the chuck to release the bits and said that it was on the English rather than the Scottish side. Beyond that he couldn't say.

Next we looked at the moulding planes. The best looking of the set were a pair of match planes used for cutting tongues and grooves in ¾-

inch boards, and a 1½-inch skew rabbet plane for cutting shoulders into wood. These were stamped:

E.FLINT
ALEXANDER

We could find nothing on Flint in any of our books. Jay suggested that I call on Emil Pollak, an authority on American wooden planes and their makers, to see if this name had surfaced recently. I reached Emil late that night. Neurosurgeons could take a lesson from the detail with which he had me describe the planes to him. He searched his files, but E. Flint was not there—yet. Flint must have been a woodworker living in Alexander, somewhere, and long labor with early census data could probably turn him up.

Two other moulding planes, a combined bead and quarter round and a ⅞-inch side-stop dado plane, were so similar to the ones marked Flint/Alexander that I was sure that they were made by the same hand. They were, however, unmarked. The bead/round plane had a knotty flaw in it—which could account for the maker's reluctance to lay claim to it. Such unstamped tools could usually be had at a considerable discount.

The screw arm plow plane was also marked E. Flint/Alexander. The five remaining irons were stamped W. BUTCHER, surmounted by a crown flanked with the letters W and R. Jay flipped open a dictionary to find that William IV had reigned as King of England from 1830 to 1837. The WR was William Rex, son of King George III.

But although they were English irons, the planemaker himself was probably a subject of Andrew Jackson, president of the twenty-four United States of America. To Jay's educated eye, these planes had a distinctly American look. English steel and American wood. Jay said this was the combination to expect. Americans could not then compete with the English edge-tool makers, but as the remaining planes showed, Yankees were on the move.

The next three moulding planes, a number 8 hollow, a number 18 round, and a number 18 hollow, bore the legend:

Two irons were stamped BUTCHER, but the number 18 hollow was stamped NEWBOULD CAST STEEL, with a detailed crown motif. All three planes had successive owners' initials R. N. and T.L. stamped into them. The maker, Truman J. McMaster, manufactured planes in the New York state prison at Auburn from 1825 to 1829 using convict labor.

The last moulding plane, a 6/8 astragal, was stamped:

Union Factory was begun by Hermon Chapin near New Haven, Connecticut, in 1826. He contracted with numerous planemakers to produce work under his mark and was the first to use power machinery to manufacture planes. Standardized power precision brought Chapin's prices down, putting his planes in many a craftsman's tool chest.

All of the moulding planes, then, seemed to be American made from the 1830s. Jay shared my delight in finding such a tight chronological grouping. But there was more.

Largest of the bench planes was a single-ironed jointer, 26 inches long and armed with a 2⅝-inch-wide Butcher iron with an unusual bell-like emblem. The clipped corner top profile of the iron was mushroomed from rough adjustment with a hammer. On the front end grain was one of my favorite marks—the trace of a bump against the sharp teeth of a bench stop.

Three of the big, handled planes had smaller counterparts in three of the moulding planes; a 2½-inch-wide, skew-ironed "jack" rabbet plane and a pair of plank or match planes for working tongues and grooves in 1¼-inch stock. The rabbet plane had an unusual side-tilted handle. The wear marks on the sole of the tonguing plane showed that it had indeed been used on five-quarter stock.

A 2-inch-wide panel-raising plane had still another variant of the w. BUTCHER stamp, this one with two sunbursts over the words WAR-RANTED—CAST STEEL. Just ahead of the skewed iron was a simple inset knife-iron to precut the cross grain and prevent splintering. Joiners use this size of plane in making paneled doors, shutters, and wainscot.

Inside the front of the chest was a rack fitted to hold an orderly array of chisels and gouges. The surviving paring chisels (there were spaces for thirteen) were tang-ended, handled with turned beech, and fitted with ferrules of brazed copper. They were stamped with the mark of w^m ASH & CO. One of Jay's books placed him in Sheffield from 1825 to 1852. The largest (2 inches wide) and the smallest (⅛ inch wide) chisels were among the few that survived.

The rack had half-moon spaces for a dozen gouges, but again only the largest, a Butcher 1½ inch, and a few others remained. It and the others were sharpened out-cannel, with the bevel on the convex side. This is what one might prefer for carving, but not for the paring and scribing of joinery, where the bevel must be in-cannel. Wondering at the gouges

Looking down on the moulding planes in their rack (left to right): *smooth, dado, Chapin astragal, three McMaster hollow and rounds, bead and round, Flint match planes (for tongue and groove) and rabbet. Below them rest the panel-raising plane* (left), *the plow plane* (center), *and the skew "jack" rabbet* (right).

The "plank" planes used to make tongue-and-groove flooring.

brought me back to my original question. Who was the man that owned this chest? What did he do? The purchased tools told when, but the tools that he made with his own hands would tell about the man.

Back at the shop, I searched the chest for more clues. In the chest were four handmade gauges—quality workmanship in rosewood, beech, and brass. Amid the trash in the chest were the raw pieces of rosewood stock for making the gauges. If finding the stock were not enough of a hint, the treatment of the scratching point of the gauges confirmed that they were all made by the same hand. Each point was centered in a ³⁄₁₆-inch-diameter hole with a slotted dowel sandwiching the blade. The panel gauge, the flooring gauge, and the common gauge all had this same pattern.

Besides the stock for making the gauges, I also found rejected parts from two of the gauges. The beam of the rosewood common gauge was protected from the set screw by a sort of notched pad. A similar but slightly less well fitted pad was sitting in one of the drawers. Unless it was for another gauge, it was rejected because it was a tiny fraction of an inch too loose a fit. The important point, however, was that finding the stock and the rejected parts in the chest was evidence that the man who made the gauges also owned the chest.

The slitting gauge bore the only hand-cut initials of the lot, a stylized *E A* on the side of the fence. This spectacular gauge bears a knife blade instead of a scratcher, and is used to cut out thin pieces of wood, such as the bottoms of the trays and drawers in the chest. I found a roller just like the one used in this gauge in one of the drawers. It was apparently rejected because it had an off-center hole. Wear on the beam of the

The surviving chisels and gouges resting in their partially disassembled rack.

gauge showed use at no specific width, but rather ·an even fading of scratches to about 8 inches.

The panel gauge (used to mark out wide parallel stock) did show wear at a specific setting, exactly 10¼ inches. This happens to be the exact width of the panels of the door to the room in which I now sit.

The flooring gauge (also called a clapboard gauge) consisted of an arm attached to a triangular block with twenty numbered steps on it. By using these steps as the fence, settings of from 4 to 8 inches are immediately available. The only marks on the tool beyond the roughly penciled numbers were the tooth marks of a twelve-point saw blade. I tried the dovetail saw from the chest in it; the teeth fit exactly into place. The marks could have been made by accident when they were stored together, or they could indicate that the saw was used to make this gauge.

Several smaller rosewood "jump-over" gauges were also in the chest. They were notched so that they could extend over a protrusion on the work being gauged. They must have been made for flooring. One of the gauges was set at 1½ inches and the other at 1¼—both common thicknesses for floorboards—and, indeed, wear on the bottom of the tonguing plane showed that it had been used on such stock.

The importance of a jump-over gauge for flooring needs some explanation. The old process of laying flooring required that the thickness be gauged only after the tongues and grooves were plowed. Nicholson described the process in 1816. Floorboards "should first be planed on their best face, and set out to season till the natural sap is quite exhausted; they may then be planed smooth, shot and squared upon one edge: the opposite edges are brought to a breadth, with a flooring gauge;

The gauges in the tray, probably made by the owner of the chest during the building boom of the early 1830s and perhaps abandoned in the economic depression that followed.

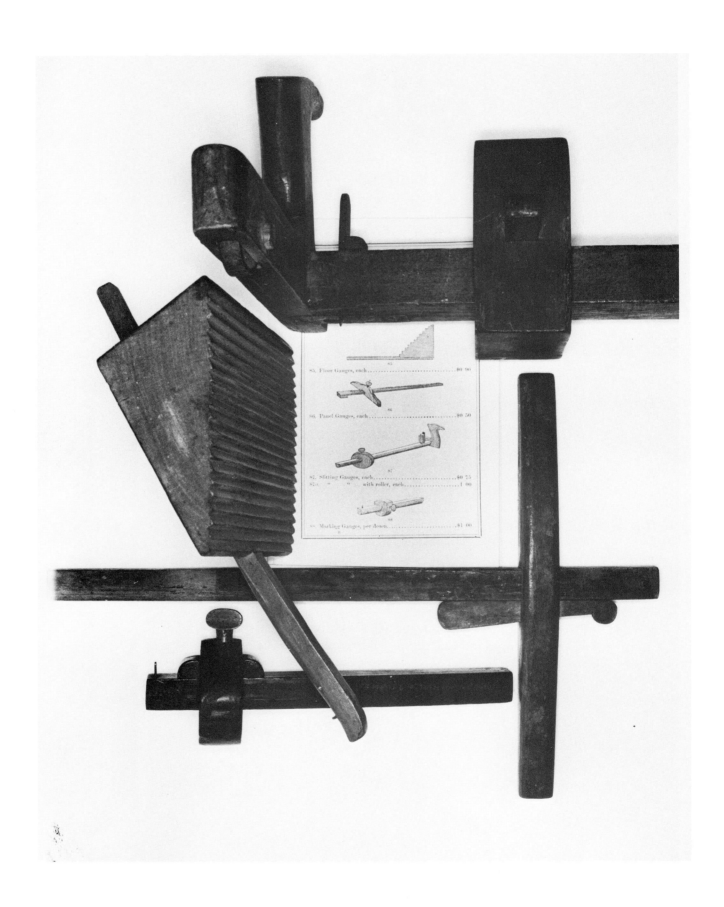

they are then gauged to thickness with a common gauge, and rebated down on the back to the lines drawn by the gauge." The rabbeted edges of the underside of each board serve as depth indicators for the floor-layer as he adzes the board to the final thickness only at the points where it crosses joists. When the carpenter prepares such flooring, the tongue and groove must be planed in before the thickness is gauged or else the planing would obliterate the gauging. Thus the need for a jump-over gauge that can reach over a tongue.

So who was he? I cannot tell you his name; the best I can do is the initials *E A* from the slitting gauge. But from the tools in the chest, the broad axe, the adze, and the boring machine, he must have been a carpenter-joiner, a skilled and competent workman living in America in the 1830s. He knew his trade well by the time he bought these tools. But how did he develop his skills when his tools showed such little use? Perhaps he had just finished his apprenticeship, and these were the tools of his first job as a journeyman. From the wear left on the tools by his work, I would guess that he laid a floor, built a door, paneled a room—and then, for whatever reason, never picked up his tools again.

YOUR OWN

I was disappointed not to find the plane used to make the grecian ovalo mouldings on the skirt around the bottom of this chest. It and many other tools must have been lost overboard in the chest's century-and-a-half voyage. The real surprise was that so many did survive, and those that did are more than enough to make another tool chest. You need gauges and planes to measure and shape the boards, saws and chisels to cut lap and dovetail joints—and you need the wood to work with.

You need wide boards to make a chest, and when a woodworker finds some wide boards, he goes after them. This wide-board imperative can lead to moral dilemmas. Two years ago my brother was loading his truck with cut-offs from a woodworking factory that had offered them free to anyone who wanted to haul them away for kindling. Halfway down in the mountain of chunks he found a big board. It was mildewed and water stained, but 12 feet long and 22 inches wide. Beneath it was another just like it; he pulled it free and uncovered another. He kept pulling until he had a pile of fifteen damp but very wide boards. Now these boards were obviously not scrap like the other scrap, but they were in the scrap pile, which made them scrap nonetheless. It was also obvious that if he didn't take them, one of the other pile-pickers would. My brother is too well raised to acquire anything by dishonest means, but he's not stupid either.

In any event, that was some time ago. The factory burned down a few weeks later, and my brother had to leave the county for unrelated reasons. He gave the boards to me, asking that I make a tool chest for him. And so I did.

The "jump-over" or "grasshopper" gauge used to mark thickness on tongue-and-groove flooring.

[opposite]
The four gauges frame their counterparts in the D. Barton tool catalog of 1873.

A small dovetailed poplar chest.

This is a little dovetailed chest with a paneled lid, skirted bottom, and sliding trays within. And that is the order to make it in: dovetail the sides, make the top and bottom to fit, and then put in the trays. You may need to glue up some boards in order to have some that are wide enough. Glued-up boards should be just as strong as single wide ones, but to be sure, I always take care that the seam on one side of the chest does not meet the seam on the other.

JOINING UP WIDE BOARDS

Fitting boards together so that "they shall seem one intire Piece" is Joseph Moxon's 1678 definition of the "Art of Joinery." Planes are the essential tools for edge joining, but without stabilized wood the best

The Little Chest

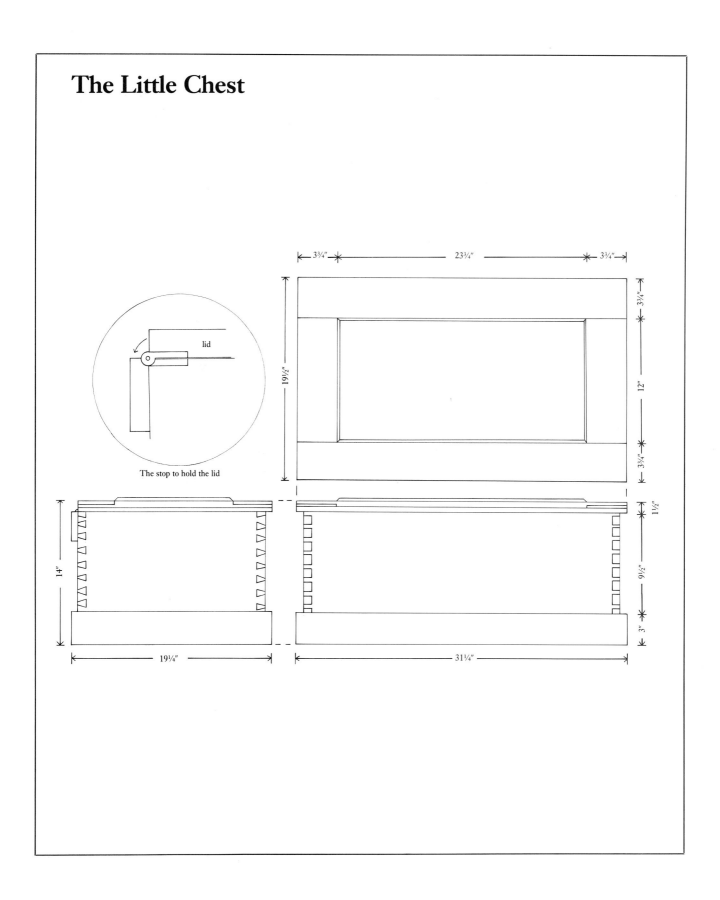

The stop to hold the lid

planes can do little good. You often need to plane the wood twice, "for it has been observ'd," says the 1734 *Builder's Dictionary* that "though Boards have lain in an House ever so long, and are ever so dry, yet when they are thus shot and planed, they will shrink afterwards beyond Belief." Only after this initial planing and redrying, when the boards "will shrink no more," may they "be again shot with good Joints."

Think about the orientation of the grain of the boards that you join together. The annual ring pattern on the end grain will tell you how the board will respond to changes in moisture content. Ideally, these rings will be at consistent right angles to the face of the boards. This "quarter-sawn" stock will not distort with further drying. Arching rings on the end grain, however, indicate boards that will become concave toward the bark side of the tree. Knowing that this will happen with such stock, you can minimize the cumulative effect by placing the boards in an alternating sequence of heart up and heart down. This will give you an undulating, wavelike but generally level surface. In a surface of all heart-up wood each board adds to the deviation of the previous one. Such an arrangement does, however, allow you to save wood because there will be less exposed sapwood to trim off for a good color match.

In 1755 Williamsburg cabinetmaker Anthony Hay placed an advertisement in the *Virginia Gazette* informing subscribers that, among other cabinetmaker's tools, he was selling "glue jointers." The glue jointer is the long plane, as long as the workbench is tall, that shoots the perfectly straight edges that you need to make the rubbed glue edge joint. If you have ever encountered the remarkable bond created when two wet panes of glass are rubbed together, then you know how the rubbed joint works. The glue bonds the joint even before it sets. The glue jointer's job is to make the edges of the boards as smooth and flat as glass.

The length of the plane serves to ride the cutting iron over hollows in the wood, cutting the high places lower and lower until there are no high places left. When you joint boards, you must put pressure on the nose of the plane at the beginning of the stroke, the tail of the plane at the end of the stroke, and evenly in the middle of the stroke. The length of the plane will eliminate hollows in the board, the shaving emerging in one long, unbroken strip. The only inaccuracy the jointer will commonly allow is gentle crowning. When you place boards with crowned edges together, they will pivot around the middle of their joint. The ends of the boards should drag when the joint is pivoted, and no light should be visible between them.

Simple tricks are the best when they are easier to do than to explain. Edge joining is like this. It is a simple fact that when the edges of two flat boards clamped face to face in the vise are planed as one, the boards are automatically aligned in a level plane when their edges are folded together. Basically, to whatever degree the plane is tilted (and it always is), an equal but opposite error is imparted to both pieces. When the two pieces are folded together, the errors cancel each other out, the boards are flat, and the joint is tight.

As demonstrated in this double exposure, the angular error in planing the two boards side by side is canceled when they are folded out to make a single wide board.

When the planing is right, the glue can do its job. Warm the board if you are using glue from the hot pot. Place one board edge-up in the vise, the edge of the other touching it, and brush the glue on both surfaces at once. Fold the joint closed and rub the two surfaces together until you feel them take hold. Check the alignment and then carefully set them aside to dry overnight propped against the wall. You don't need to use dowels—the joint will be plenty strong. If you want reinforcement after the glue has set, however, heed once more the *Builders Dictionary* and "let every Joint be secured by two Wooden Dovetails, let in cross the Joint on the Backside." Dovetails, or "butterfly" insets, within your chest show class; use them and your tools won't speak ill of you.

Inset "butterflies" across the grain.

DOVETAILING

Like so many operations in joinery, success in dovetailing depends on accurately bringing the material true and square. Without this to build upon, the rest of your work will be as useless as barking at a knot. See that your stock is right before you go on.

1. Find your gauge (the old scantillion) and set it to a bit more ($\frac{1}{16}$ inch) than the thickness of the boards. This extra measure will be planed off the completed joint. Now run the fence of the gauge against the end grain of each of the boards to scratch the extent of the tails and pins all the way around the two ends of each of the four boards. The length of common dovetails is determined by the thickness of the wood. The width, however, is a matter of taste and tradition. I will say only that you should not make the pins and tails the same size—that is what machines do.

Lay out and saw (but don't chisel) the tails first.

2. Dividers or a diagonally placed ruler will give an even spacing to the dovetails. When you have spaced them as you wish, take a try square and, at each point, extend two lines spaced about ¼ inch apart across the end grain. These lines are the distance between the ends of the tails. The lines that border the space between them diverges from these points down to the base. This angle is easily set on an adjustable bevel by laying it against a square so that in 6 inches of length it deviates 1 inch from a right angle. You need to draw these lines only on the face side of the

[opposite above]
Transfer the dimensions to the adjoining board.

[opposite below]
Saw on the "waste" side of the piece.

boards. Careful sawing will ensure that they are true on the back side as well. (If you saw the tails in pairs then it is wise to lay out the stock more fully.) Mark the waste to be removed with xs so there can be no mistake. It has happened before to better folk than you and I.

3. Saw the diagonals of these lines first, then bring the saw around to cut square. The short length of the cuts can be done quickly with even your finest saw. (The eighteenth-century Seaton tool chest held a dovetail saw with 20 teeth to the inch, measuring 18 thousandths of an inch thick.) The saw cuts for the tails determine the size of the pins.

4. Set the sawn but unchiseled tail board on the end grain of the pin board. Take the saw and set it in the kerfs, drawing it back hard enough to leave a good mark on the underboard. Don't cut, just mark into the wood. Be sure that the two pieces don't move until all the marks are made.

5. Now take the try square again and extend straight lines back down the face side. *Think* and mark the waste areas to be removed with xs. Saw these from the face side, cutting on the *waste* side of the line. Too much on the waste side and you will have to pare away and trim before the joints will fit; too close, and the joint will be too loose.

6. Check the edge on your chisels—they need to be sharp. Set the chisel a bit inside the waste area from the line scratched with the gauge. Drive it straight down, pull it out, and then dig back to it with the bevel still facing the end grain of the board. Cut halfway through from one side and then turn the board over and finish from the other side. The narrowing spaces between the pins may have to be done entirely from the wide side. See that the wood is well supported underneath so that it does not splinter out. Check the joints to see that they will fit properly before you apply the glue. Put the four sides together and check them with a square before they set up.

SKIRTS AND BOTTOMS

When you have the four boards dovetailed into a box sitting before you, most of the work is done. While you have the tools out, though, make the skirt around the bottom because it is dovetailed too. For extra strength, run the skirt joints the opposite way from the box joints: if the short sides of the box got the tails, give the short sides of the skirt pins. The top edge of the dovetails will look best with a mitered dovetail. If you wish, the skirt can add considerable depth to the chest. My wheeled chest has side boards only 11 inches wide, but the skirt extends the depth another 3 inches. I joined the skirt and sides with long interlocking grooves plowed along their edges. It will be a long time before they come apart.

The bottom can be set within the rectangle of the side boards, or you can gain another inch of depth by matching it to the outside dimension of the box and then letting the skirt slip down around it. Glue and nails will hold the bottom in, but the strongest bottoms are inset, somewhat like

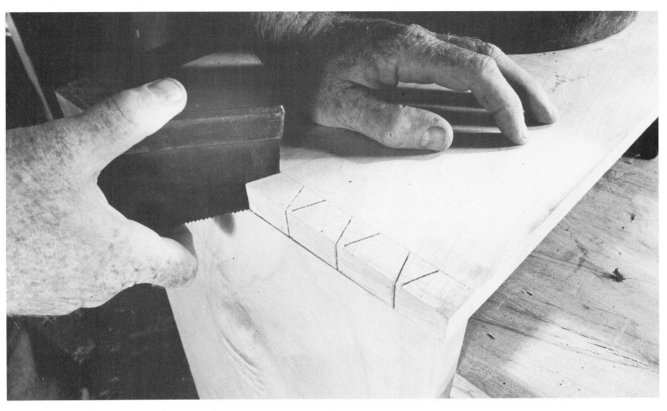

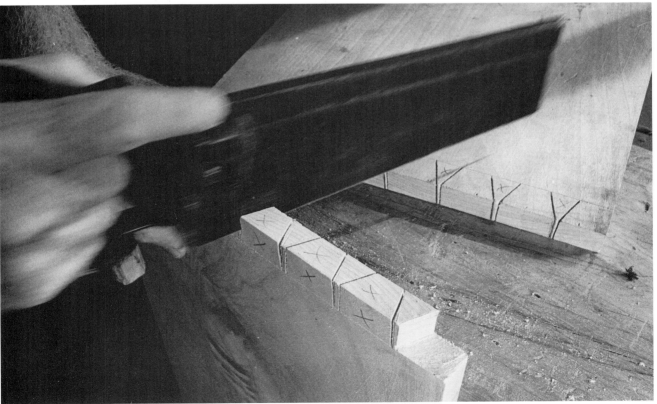

[above]
Chisel out the remainder.

[right]
Miter the top dovetail of the skirt.

panels in a door. If you do this, be sure to modify the dovetails to accommodate the groove plowed through them.

THE LID

A tool chest is intended to protect the tools. Getting caught in a rainstorm on the job is a lot less worrisome when your tool chest is built right. This lid is designed to shed water and to stay tight regardless of changes in humidity. The top is made up of a frame which holds a panel and a lip attached around the underside to stiffen it and fit around the upper edge of the chest.

Cut the four boards that comprise the frame to their proper lengths (plus a bit) and plane them square and true. Mark the top faces and the outer edges. The inside edges of the boards may now be prepared to accept the grooved panel. This entails cutting a shoulder, or rabbet, into the lower inside edges of all four pieces. Gauge down a quarter inch from the upper, face side of the frame boards on all of the pieces. This quarter inch is the wood that must remain as a tongue to fit into the groove around the panel. The wood that needs to be removed for a depth of ⅜ inch (also laid out with the gauge) can be dealt with by a rabbet plane or a chisel.

The rabbeting complicates the half-lap joints of the corners of the frame. The best way to deal with this is just to cut the tongue off in the area of the joints and start with a clean slate. Set the long boards on top of the short ends as they will be situated in the finished lid. Mark the long boards at the inner corner where they intersect the short boards. Make saw cuts through the tongue on the long boards at this point and then cut away the tongue to the ends of the boards. Now the lapping can proceed.

For the half lap, set the gauge at half the thickness of the wood (⅜ inch) and, always fencing the gauge from the top, face side, mark around the ends of all four boards. Scribe across the grain where the edges of the boards cross each other, first testing the alignment for squareness. Mark the waste (the lower half of the long ends, the upper half of the short ends) with big *X*s and saw the wood away. It will be a perfect fit.

Make the panel to fit the frame. The groove around the perimeter of the panel can easily be cut with a plow plane or a quarter-inch grooving plane. But it can also be easily cut with a sharp chisel. Lay out the width of the groove (the middle quarter of the ¾-inch thickness) with the gauge. Start at the far end of one of the long-grain sides with the bevel of the chisel down. Work your way backwards, rolling out curls until you have gone in half an inch. On the end grain you need to reverse the procedure and work with the bevel up; start at the near end and slowly work away from you. A sharp chisel is the secret of success.

When you assemble the top, glue and screw the corner joints, but leave the panel free. As the *Builder's Dictionary* noted, "This will give Liberty to the Board to shrink and swell." If you glued it in place, it would

Half-lap the frame of the lid, maintaining the tongue for the central panel.

"so restrain the Motion of the Wood, that it cannot shrink without tearing." Leave the panel loose and it will "last a long Time, without either parting in the Joints, or splitting in the Wood."

Screw the lip to the underside of the lid with common butt miters at the corners. The lip needs to fit around the top with enough clearance that it can be closed as it swings in the arc. You may also want to make a rim for this lip to mate with. It may be made in the same manner as the

The groove around the central panel can be quickly cut with a chisel.

skirt, but in any case needs to be securely fastened to the case, as it is an obvious place to grab the chest to lift it.

A chest from the nineteenth century is happy with butt hinges on it. They began to replace the strap hinge in the mid-eighteenth century. I once explored the ruins of a house built about this time in which every door was hung on butt hinges screwed to the surface like the old-fashioned strap hinges. A chain or a hinged iron strap will keep the lid

On the road again.

from falling clean over when you open it, or you can have the back edge of the lid strike a bar fastened across the back of the chest.

Old chests can look as common as an old shoe on the outside and yet be beautifully inlaid masterpieces on the inside. I am happy with simple open trays that slide back and forth to let you get to the bottom of the chest. If you decide to make two trays to a tier, be sure to make each no wider than one-third of the interior width of the chest. I made the trays of my wheeled chest a bit too wide, and it is a tight squeeze between the trays when I need to get something out from the bottom.

THE LITTLE TOOL BOX

The traditional carpenter's tool carrier is a basket carried over the shoulder by means of a stick thrust through its handles. I do not know when the open wooden tool box came into general use. It appears in several early nineteenth-century photographs, but only rarely in line drawings.

Perhaps it is one of those things that is there, but the artist wishes was not.

I have put many a mile on my tool box. It is not old, but one that I made after an example from Duplin County, North Carolina. I have used it on jobs around the country and have had to rebuild it only once. That was when one of my fellow carpenters fell off of the roof of a privy and landed right on top of it. Fortunately, it was almost empty of tools; so the tool box was hurt more than he was.

I have an old manual training book from 1916 entitled *Problems in Farm Woodwork*. A tool box (they call it a tool carrier) like mine is one of the first projects in the book. It is made low so that "it will easily slide under the seat of a buggy." The angled sides are connected with what the book called "hopper joints," after the agricultural fashion.

Weight is an important consideration on an item like this. The sides and bottom are half-inch pine; the center handle is of inch-thick stock. Only one of the sides should flare out if you do a lot of walking. The other face, which is against your leg, is better kept square. If you don't carry your toolbox for long distances, though, flare at will.

Make your tool box long enough for your handsaws to fit in it, about 32 inches. The bottom of the box is about 8 inches wide and the sides are 6 inches tall. The angle of the splay on my box is 3 inches in 5; that is, I set the adjustable bevel so that when its body is held flat against one side of a square, the blade of the bevel crosses the 3-inch mark on one arm and the 5-inch mark on the other. Saw the ends of the boards to this angle and then plane their bottom edges to the same angle. Glue and nail the sides together and then inset the bottom, planing its edges to the appropriate angles for a tight fit. This is the sort of bevel work used so often in boat building.

Fit the center board for the handle last. My handle does not reach to the bottom, which is not the normal case. I wanted to save weight and add room, but it really makes things more of a jumble. The handle hole is simply two auger holes with the wood in between chiseled out. Making this handle hole about three times longer than the width of your hand will prove a great timesaver. When the tools are out of balance, you only need to shift your hand position to find harmony with the load you bear.

6 CHAIRS

If it isn't baroque—don't fix it.
—William Weldon

I like chairmaking. Chairs are intimate objects. You might say, "I love that desk!" or "I love that table!" but you only mean it when you say, "I love that chair!" As one old chairmaker put it, a good chair is "like somebody hugging you."

The three chairs in this chapter represent three quite different styles. My instructions for each are correspondingly different to match the varying degrees of control required. They are all good forms for the first-time chairmaker. The materials and techniques range from nailed willow twigs to compound beveled ancient white oak. The work can be challenging as well as surprising. The freedom afforded by the rustic form can be far more demanding of the craftsman than the rigorous precision required to join the wainscot chair.

RUSTIC CHAIRS

Every few decades the wheel of fashion turns again to a peculiar style of furniture known as "rustic." This style, contrived to combine the comforts of civilization with the look of wildness, can be remarkably varied and sophisticated. Far from being the simple constructs of close-to-nature country folk, the rustic chairs of the eighteenth century were actually carved from solid wood to look like gnarled sticks and bark.

Originally, only the very rich suffered from nature deprivation, but as over-civilization afflicted more and more people, rustic furniture became increasingly popular. Someone eventually thought of using real sticks with the bark on them instead of carving and painting blocks of beech. This opened up rustic furniture making to anyone equipped with a hatchet and some nails. People even began making rustic work as a pastime. A woman's magazine of 1857 recommended using idle time in the winter, "when there is but little to do in the garden," to cut wood for "making rustic chairs and tables." My own grandfather made bent willow chairs in Celtic convolutions as a sideline during the Great Depression.

Although rural and amateur furniture making continued unabated, commercially manufactured designs soon appeared. In about 1900 the Old Hickory Chair Company in Indiana began more than a half century of manufacturing simple, comfortable, inexpensive, straight-ahead hickory chairs. These chairs quickly became the dominant species in the summer camps of America. Their uniformity is remarkable; the hickory saplings were grown like corn just for chairmaking, harvested, and set into identical bending frames. The tenons to form the joints and the rounded ends were shaped by lathes and tools that resembled giant electric pencil sharpeners.

Above all, though, rustic furniture is fun. Your designs can be as free as the material you make it with. Strict instructions for this kind of work defeat the purpose. I can, however, offer some suggestions on materials, methods, and tools; the rest I leave to you and the trees.

Classic bent-willow plant stand from the 1920s.

WOOD

Winter is the hunting season for wood for rustic work. If you want the bark to stay on the sticks, you must cut them when the leaves are off. In spring and summer, when trees are growing and the cells between the bark and the wood are dividing rapidly, the bark will come off with little provocation.

Hickory is the most common species for joined chairs, and willow for nailed work. Every region has its own style based on the material at hand. I like to find pieces that have natural bends and crooks that I can exploit in the design. More often, though, the pieces dictate the design. Creek banks are the place to look for saplings with right-angle bends at their bases. A dump frequented by landscapers is a good place to visit after a winter storm. I literally stumbled across a place in the woods filled with wonderful material. A sawdust pile from an old mill had rotted away, exposing the roots of the saplings that had grown on it.

BENDING

If you want to, you can bend a living tree, tie it, and let it grow into the desired curve for a season before cutting it. It is a strange sight to see, though—a tree bent double and tied with rope. Passers-by feel bad about it and usually let it go.

Green hickory bends easily and holds its shape when it dries. Think of the forest as a blacksmith's fire. When you pull a tree from the forest, it is easily bent like red hot iron from the fire. But, just as the iron cools, the wood dries and becomes set in its new shape. You must strike while the wood is green. If necessary, though, winter-cut wood, green or dry, can be steamed for bending. Green wood responds faster to steaming, but must stay in a bending form longer than dry wood before it is set. The simplest steamer made from a length of pipe set on the end of a teakettle will do the trick.

DESIGN

I have never tried to copy existing designs in rustic furniture, although this could certainly be worthwhile. Frankly, the rustic work that I do is intended to please myself and not a potential customer. You will find that the natural forms that you discover will suggest many designs to you. I take great pleasure in standing up various combinations and trying to evaluate them before the precarious pile falls apart.

[opposite]
Joined hickory chair and a nailed bent-willow rocker.

Trussing hickory in the wintertime.

JOINING

Much "gypsy" furniture is simply nailed together. This will do for tables and stands, but except in willow work, which has enough small pieces fastened by enough nails, a nailed-together chair will not last long. To endure, the joints of a chair need the passionate embrace of mortice and tenon joints. The obvious way to cut these joints would be to bore a hole in one piece and whittle the end of the other down to fit in it. Much work was once done this way, but since at least the eighteenth century chair tenons have been shaped by rotary cutting. Most pieces can be mounted in a lathe and the tenons quickly turned. Awkward pieces can be shaped with variations of the wheelwright's "hollow auger."

The name "hollow auger" is apt. Like an auger, it shaves away everything around a central core which remains to form the tenon. Wheelwright's spoke-tenoning tools can still be found, but you can also make your own out of wood. Basically, it is a turned hickory shaft; one end fits into the brace for turning it and the other is bored hollow with a steel blade positioned to plane away the wood as it turns.

Although rustic chairs are highly individualistic, the joints are uniformly machined. The tenons on the main frame of a chair should be at least ¾ inch in diameter. These primary mortice and tenon joints need to be further secured with glue and nails. If you make the two sides of the chair first, you can bore the holes for the tenons of the front and back rails so that they slightly intersect the side joints. This locks the sides of the chair against pulling loose.

Another general consideration is to see that the front stretcher that frames the seat is set below the stretchers on the sides. If you do this, the seat will be comfortable; if you do not, your legs will fall asleep after five minutes of sitting.

The traditional auger for chairmakers is the spoon bit. It allows you to get close to the far side of the post without the lead screw of a twist auger poking through. Be warned, though; when a spoon bit shows on the other side, it ain't no little hole.

BARK BOTTOMS

Winter-made rustic chairs are traditionally bottomed with spring-harvested hickory bark. In the spring and summer the growing layer between bark and wood is easily broken. A number of trees will provide bark for seats. I know hickory, but I have seen excellent work done in ash and elm bark. Experiment and you may find others, but don't waste time barking up the wrong tree.

The process is basically the same for any bark tree: find a tree and cut it down and then pull off the bark. Cut it to the width and thickness for weaving. Obviously, taking the bark off kills the tree, but you can make good use of the wood. If you are not making any other hickory work, such

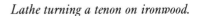

Lathe turning a tenon on ironwood.

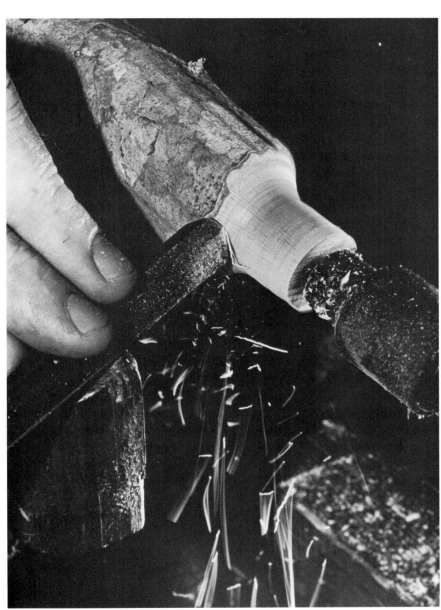

as axe helves or snowshoes, then you can at least add a lot of naked firewood in your stack.

Look for a hickory tree that runs between 6 and 10 inches in diameter. Smaller trees have thinner bark, sometimes too thin. Try to find a tree with few knots that tends towards the cylindrical rather than tapering heavily. Chop the tree down and cut the top end off at the point where you figure it becomes too small or knotty. This will determine the maximum length of your weaving strips. I strip the bark off the tree immediately, but I understand that if you let the tree lie for about a week first, the bark will hold its light color instead of turning brown.

A spoke pointer and hand- and factory-made tenon cutters for problem joints.

STRIPPING

Prop the log up on its stump and, with a drawknife, shave off the outer rough, hard, scaly bark on the top side of the tree. Cut just deep enough to get through to the light colored stuff. Now take your pocketknife and cut along the grain down the length of the tree to divide the bark into strips. If the woods are pleasant (no mayflies), you may want to cut the strips to their final width, about ¾ to 1 inch. If, however, you want to get back to the shop sooner, cut the strips from 4 to 8 inches wide and cut them smaller when you get home.

When you have cut the bark on the tree to the width that you want, pry one end of the bark free from the wood and slowly pull it off down the length of the tree. Watch for snags and be ready to cut them free with your knife. Roll the strips around your hand as you go and hitch the end around the coil to keep it from springing loose. (Speaking of springs, you can also take the bark off of the tree in one piece by slitting it down one side and prying it loose. When the bark is free, it returns to a pipelike cylinder. This hickory pipe was traditionally used to run water from a spring to a whiskey still.)

When you have to cut broad bands of bark into narrower strips, a

Drawknife off the rough outer bark of the hickory.

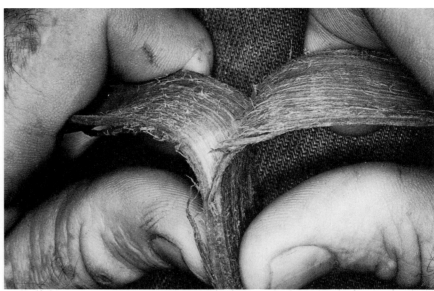

[above]
Cut along the grain and pull off the strips of inner bark.

[right]
Split the bark in half.

cutting gauge is a big help. This can be a regular joiner's cutting gauge or one that you make up expressly for cutting seating strips. The blades for such a gauge need to be very hard and thin. Bits of old clock spring make excellent blades for just this reason: they will hold an edge against the miles of hickory, yet are thin enough to pass easily through it.

Although many people use the bark just as it is stripped from the tree, I always split it into half of its initial thickness and weave only with the inner part. Some people split the bark but use both halves, including the outer, brittle stuff. The splitting technique is the same as that used for working white oak sapwood into splits. Take one end and work your knife into it lengthwise, giving the knife a twist to open the split. Now take a half in each hand and work the split down the length of the strip. Should one of the sides start to get thicker than the other, pull more sharply on it to bend it more than the other and make the split run evenly again.

As the bark coils dry, they turn a deep brown color. Even holding them in your hands you would mistake them for leather. Hickory bark is very useful and strong. Thoreau mentioned a boat on Walden Pond that was anchored by a cable made from strips of hickory bark. Soak them in water until they are easy to work before you weave with them. Just like wood, bark swells in width when it absorbs water and will shrink back when it dries. You must beat your wet weave tight as you work to keep it from loosening too much when it dries.

WEAVING

Bark seat weaving begins with warping the chair, that is, wrapping the initial course of strips in one direction prior to the crosswise interlacing.

The bottom warped and the weave begun. Four alternating starts create the herringbone pattern.

When one strip runs out, just tie in another.

Splits of white oak and ash wood are woven the same way, but only bark is pliant enough to tie in a knot. This makes things easier right away, because the first thing you do is taper down one end of the first strip and tie it around one of the back stretchers. Bring it around under the front stretcher and loop back and around, pulling tight as you go around and around. When a strip runs out, trim down its end and that of the next piece and knot them together. Keep all of the knots on the underside. Be sure to keep the outside of the bark facing up and out. When the bark dries, it will crown and make a much more comfortable and attractive seat than the smoother-surfaced but down-cupping inside. It all works out in the end.

The finished bark bottom. Different chair—same pattern.

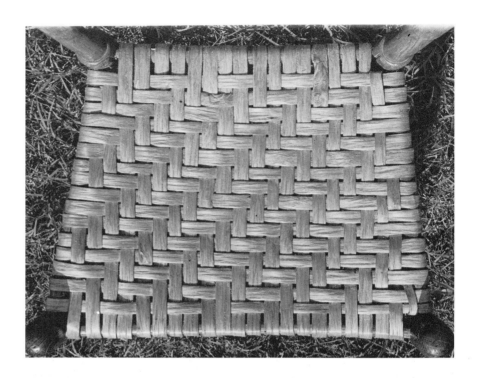

When you have wrapped the chair from front to back (or side to side), turn under and around one of the back posts and start the weave. The most common weave for strip work is the herringbone. This weave develops a regular pattern by getting out of step with itself. Each strip goes over two and under two, but starts its journey across the seat in one of four ways. The first strip starts under two, the second under one, the third over two, and the fourth over one. Repeat this sequence all the way across the chair seat and tuck the final end into the weave on the underside. Long diagonals on a seat for a century will be your reward.

THE RED CHAIR

In the folk art museum in town there is an anonymous painting of a baby in a red high chair. The posts and rungs for the chair are not as fat as those you often see in the South. Southern soft maple needs the extra diameter for strength. The only copy that I have made of this chair is in elm, partially because I like its grain and partially because I had some.

Turned chairs such as this one have been around a very long time. Turning is quicker and easier than carving, and one element of the joint, the tenon, can be shaped at the same time as the pattern. The other element is quickly made with a brace and bit. When you turn these patterns, make a light incision to mark each joint, including the ends of the mortices for the back splats. Be sure to indicate the proper offset for the stretchers that frame the seat.

To spread the base and keep baby from tipping the chair over, the four leg posts diverge at the bottom. This means that the top ends of the posts converge and that the back splats, if inserted in the normal way, would also lean inward and tend to tip baby into the oatmeal. One way to deal with this is to bend the back splats into progressively deeper curves as they go higher on the back. The back splats (split from white oak) are small enough to fit in a large cooking pot, so steaming should not present a problem. Steam them for half an hour and overbend them to allow for springback. Leave them in the form overnight. Shape the final curves and ends after they are set. A bench like Hulot's shown on page 24 is perfect for boring and assembling chairs like this one. You can use an adjustable bevel to ensure that all of your holes are bored at the same angles. I usually assemble the chair first and then mortice the back posts to accept the splats. I can eyeball the mortices to match the angles of the curved slats much better this way.

Baby in a Red Chair, *nineteenth century, anonymous (courtesy Abby Aldrige Rockefeller Folk Art Center, Williamsburg, Virginia).*

RUSH SEATS

Chair seats of woven rush have seen the south end of humanity since the days of the pharaohs. Countless different plants have been used—from corn husks to pine trees (in the form of paper-based imitation rush). The marsh-dwelling common cattail, however, makes about the best bottom a chair could have. Cattails are wild plants, growing free by the roadside, but are often adopted by someone living nearby. Ask around before you harvest too near a dwelling.

Gather your cattails when the leaf tips just start to turn brown. In our part of the country this puts you in the high weeds in August, just at the time when Mr. Copperhead is feeling hot and mean. If you make a cottonmouth angry, I hear, it will follow you all day until it bites you. My cousin Walter won't go near the marsh without a stick to beat the bushes, and he always hollers, "*Ho snake! Ho snake!*" as he goes.

It's cattail leaves, rather than flower stalks, that you want. Slice them off diagonally at the base with a sharp knife. Bundle them up and tie them loosely with one of the leaves. Set them away in a dark, cool place to dry. Give them plenty of air to prevent mildew and rot.

When the rushes are dry, the tip ends will start to frizzle and the bundle will have shrunk. The now loose binding will have fallen to the floor. Dried leaves need to be dampened with water to make them soft enough to weave without breaking. Sprinkling the bundle with rainwater and wrapping it with a damp towel may be enough. If you see that the rush is cracking, however, you may need to soak it. Overnight in a cold rain barrel or an afternoon in a warm tub will do. Try not to prepare more leaves than you can weave at one sitting; they may start to go bad if you resoak them more than once or twice. Stand them to drain awhile before you begin work.

One, two, or three strands of leaves will make up the weaving cord.

Gather ye cattails.

Springing in the splats.

Fewer leaves makes for smaller diameter cord. The smaller the cord, the finer the work and the longer it takes; the more, the fatter and coarser and faster. I would rather weave with three but sit on one.

Rush seat weaving proceeds as a spider spins her web. The weave moves from corner to corner in a converging rectangular spiral. To start, take the leaves and place them, butt end first, down inside the left-hand corner of the seat frame. Let the coarse heavy ends hang down below. There are four moves to make at each corner.

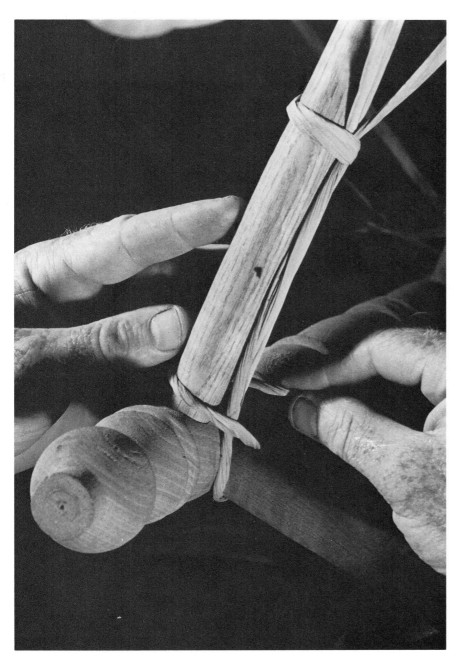

Tie the rush to one of the rungs and begin the twist and weave.

1. Towards you over the top.
2. Away from you underneath.
3. Up through the middle and over to the left.
4. Back under and shoot to the right.

After which, you rotate the chair clockwise one-quarter turn and recommence at the next corner. As you spin the chair around, wrapping the four corners of the frame, four squares of rush will grow like rope crystals to fill the space.

The pattern is the same in every corner, traced here by a beam of light.

Roll the leaves smoothly together between the length of your fingers as you go, maintaining the same direction of twist as you weave. Always make the twist toward the center of the rail that the cord is passing over. This sounds simple, but calls for mental gymnastics as the cord passes in alternate directions. If you twist toward yourself when you lay from left to right, you will need to twist away from you when going right to left.

Cattail leaves run about 5 feet long at best. This means that you must continually add new leaves to keep the cord going. Make your additions

Turn in a new leaf before the old one runs out.

Stuff the pockets with trimmings or shavings.

when the cord reaches the mid-point between two corners. To add a new leaf, stick about 6 inches of its heavy end down between the stoutest strands of the cord. Give the cord a twist or two to lock the newcomer in place and then lay it down to join in the twist with the others. You can also tie in new leaves as you go.

As the corners of the frame fill up, pound the cords with a beating stick to ensure that the weave is tight. The fat ends of the added leaves that have been growing like a beard beneath the seat can be shaved off to provide the stuffing to fill and cushion the seat. Slice them off with your knife and force them evenly into the triangular pockets with the end of the beating stick. Fine wood shavings from the plane will do as well for stuffing if your leaf butts are too coarse.

When you are working with a trapezoidal chair seat with the front rail longer than the back rail, you will need to add courses to the front corners until they are even with the back. Start as you would for a regular chair, making six complete passes around the chair, stopping just before you pass over the right side of the back rail on the last go-round. Now take some leaves to make an extra cord and tie them to the midpoint of the inner cord on the left. Weave this new cord around the front corners, and then thin and merge it with the old run which you stopped earlier. Wrap this merged cord around the chair until you reach the stopping point again. Repeat adding on the left and merging on the right until the corners line up.

On a rectangular seat, the two short sides will fill up before the long sides. Once this happens, the weave gets even simpler. Start at one side of the open space and go over and under, back and forth, as you would when writing a figure 8. Keep stuffing and beating and twisting the seating until everything is tight.

Let the newly woven seat dry in a cool, dry space away from direct sunlight.

THE WAINSCOT CHAIR

My daughter Rachel had outgrown the first chair that I had made for her, and she decided that I was to make her another. Pulling a copy of Wallace Nutting's *Furniture of the Pilgrim Century* off of the shelf, she went through the pages considering each one. She liked a turned, three-legged chair best, but was intrigued by the odd back on a more conventional four-legged wainscot chair on the facing page. The back panel of this chair was pierced with slots and holes to make a tape loom for weaving when the chair was not occupied. With due deliberation, she settled on the latter.

This seventeenth-century chair once belonged to the Robinson family of New England and is one of the few surviving examples of a wainscot chair of American origin. It is called a wainscot chair because the back is composed of one or more panels free-floating in a frame. Although the term "wainscot" later came to include the painted pine paneling of America, this chair is in the style of the original English rooms paneled with quartered white oak.

The loom fits like a panel in this little wainscot chair.

STOCK

The best wood for this chair comes from a very old white oak tree. The pieces of the frame are so small that a single fireplace-sized billet will do the entire chair. Worm holes in the wood are of no consequence. Split out all the pieces to their rough size, then square them up with the usual sequence of hatchet and plane. White oak tends to warp when a fresh surface is exposed, even when it has dried for years; so remember that a

The Wainscot Chair

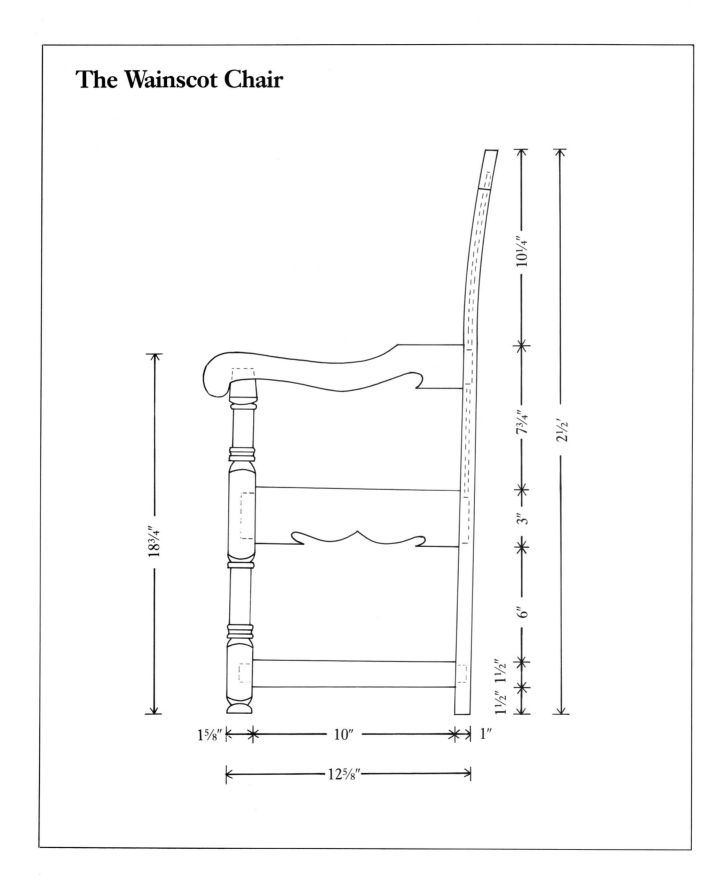

The Wainscot Chair

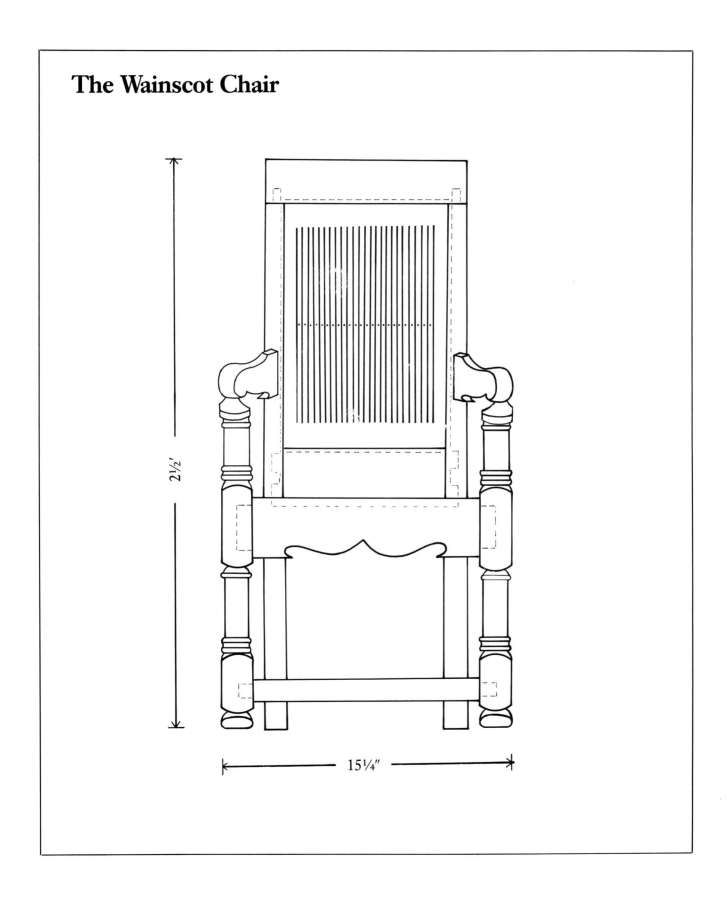

square or exact shape may not be the same from one day to the next. The small pieces for this little chair should give scant trouble, though. Also, since all the banging about that you will give the posts while you mortice them would be murder on the turnings, the lathe work must wait until the joinery is complete.

JOINING

Use a double-toothed morticing gauge to lay out the joints, both the mortices and tenons. If you do not have one, make one with two snipped-off brads driven into a shouldered wooden staff. You will need this gauge not only for the joint layout but also for the first cuts on the panel groove. The joints are all simple; even the grooves in the back posts and stretchers to house the panel are no trouble if you remember to cut them first. Should you not cut them first (by running a chisel down the grain between the scratched lines), then you may accidentally cut your mortices too long before realizing that the groove in the connecting piece has taken much of the tenon away with it.

ANGLES

The side stretchers of the chair approach the front and back posts at an angle, rather than straight on. The best approach is to cut the stretcher tenons straight but bevel their shoulders and the mortices in the posts. An adjustable bevel and a framing square will make it easy to set the angles for both sides. It's simple arithmetic. If the outside dimension of the front is 15½ inches and the back is 12½, then the difference is 3 inches. Thus, the front should extend half of this distance to one side of a right angle, or 1½ inches. If the inside of the front post is to be 10 inches away from the inside of the back post, then the angles of the chair are represented on the square by a line from the 1½-inch mark on one arm and the 10-inch mark on the other. A more convenient deviation of ¾ inch in 5 would be precisely the same angle. Lay the body of the adjustable bevel on the short measure (¾ inch) side of the square and adjust the blade until it extends from the ¾-inch mark to the 5-inch mark. This gives you both the shoulder angles of the tenons and the angles of the mortices in the posts.

To avoid confusion and save effort, lay out the length of all of the side stretchers simultaneously on their face sides. (Assuming that you are making a chair with parallel legs and that the stretchers will be of equal lengths.) From these lines you may scribe across the appropriate angles for the shoulders. Always work from the face side, using opposing ends of the bevel blade at opposing ends of the stretchers.

Now you can use the morticing gauge (at the same setting that you used to make the front and back) to lay out the mortices in the posts and

Angle the mortice and the shoulders of the tenon. In some original chairs of this type the tenon is angled and the mortice square.

the tenons on the stretchers. Saw the tenons, and use the bevel to guide the angle of your chisel as you cut the mortices in the front and back posts. The mortice passes clear through the back posts, for this is where most of the strain on a chair is concentrated. Put it all together, look at it (congratulations), and take it apart for turning.

TURNING

Mount the morticed post in the lathe, making sure that it is perfectly centered. If you are even a little bit off, you will have to reduce the diameter of the turnings excessively to eliminate all of the flats. The squareness of the stock, as opposed to the usual roundness, makes for other cautions. To prevent the corners of the square sections from being splintered away, cut their borders first. The best tool for this is the skew chisel, striking in from side to side until you have cut in to an unbroken circumference. When you have so defined a section to be turned, you can bring it to a cylinder and then turn the shapes as usual.

THE ARMS

The arms present a slightly more complex problem than the lower side stretchers. They join the back posts where they have started to slope back. This makes their shoulders a compound angle. The front ends of the arms sit on tenons cut on the tops of the front posts. Because these joints are concealed, you may allow a little more play in them to bring the back joints into alignment.

The easiest approach to determining these angles is to hold the actual arm right beside where it is to go and scribe the angles directly onto it. Cut the tenons on the tops of the front posts (canted to match the angle of the arms). Set a fully shaped arm tight up beside the chair so that the front rests on the shoulder of the tenon and the back touches the rear post at the proper elevation. Scratch the inside angle by drawing the awl or knife flat against the back post to mark the vertical angle on the arm.

Now, without moving the arm, hold a straightedge on top of the arm, flat against the face of the back post. Scribe against this and repeat underneath the arm to mark the horizontal angle of the tenon shoulders. The final line on the outer face of the arm can be found by connecting these last two lines. Before you remove the arm, sight over to the tenon on the post and inscribe the location of its mortice on the underside of the arm. Cut the joints as before.

ASSEMBLY AND KERFING IN

Although you have used exceptional care and skill in cutting the joints for the chair, you may occasionally discover on final assembly that there is more than a needle scratch to show where the junctions are. There is another path to perfection if you miss it on the first try. First, pull the joints tight with clamps or twisted ropes. Then use a fine tenon saw and recut the shoulders of each of the tenons with the sawblade riding against the sides of the posts. This "kerfing in" will make all shoulders parallel and equidistant from their destinations. When you pull the joints to-

Draw up each frame with a twisted cord and "kerf in" the tenon shoulders with a fine-toothed saw.

gether again, they should be perfect. If they are not, repeat until they are. Watch out for tenons that have bottomed out in their mortices and couldn't go any deeper if they wanted to. Drawbore and peg all joints except those on top where the loom back goes in.

Kerfing the loom. Bend it, saw it, and straighten it out.

THE LOOM

What makes this chair special is the rigid heddle tape loom of alternating holes and slots. You will need a smooth, hard wood to make the loom (Laplanders use either reindeer bone or antler); the threads will catch and wear on rough stuff. For chair back looms or those that will be used by children, strength and split resistance are most important. I use elm. I ripped some ¾-inch elm boards in half to ⅜ inch thick and then planed them to a smooth ¼ inch.

The loom for Rachel's chair has twenty-two slots and twenty-three holes spaced at intervals of ³⁄₁₆ inch. Drilling the holes is no trouble; just be sure to burnish or burn them smooth inside so that they will not wear out the threads. The slots can be cut surprisingly easily by placing the point of your hand saw on the line and cutting as well as you can until you break through. Once the blade reaches through to the other side, the sawing is easy.

I overcomplicated the job of slot cutting by steaming the thin wood and then bending it so that it could be sawn from the side. Resteaming allowed the wood to straighten out, and also released the tensions inherent in the wood. This sent the ribbons of wood twisting and leaning into each other. It was a cute trick though and makes a good story when someone mentions the little chair by the hearth with the loom in the back.

7 DOMESTIC DEVICES

As other people have a sign
I say—just stop and look at mine!
Here Wratten, cooper, lives and makes
Ox bows, trug baskets and hay rakes.
Sells shovels both for flour and corn
And shauls and makes a good box churn
Trenchers too, for use at dinners.
I make and mend both tub and cask
And hoop 'em strong to make them last.
Here's butter prints and butter scales.
And butter boards and milking pails. . . .

—Fifteenth-century signboard from Sussex, England

WHETHER for coin, for friendship, or just to pass the time, making woodenware for the home has a special advantage—it gets you in good with the cook. This work defies pigeonholing into a specific profession. Some was done by the cooper, some by the carpenter, some by the turner; but most was done by someone around the house who had the time and the inclination to work in a corner by the fire making this or that, knowing that the work would be rewarded with a pie—or better. What follows is a short cookbook of some of my favorite recipes in domestic woodwork.

SPOONS

The mountain valley in New Mexico where we used to live kept us rich in scenery but poor in the pocketbook. When one of the women had a birthday coming, some of the men would look for aspen or cottonwood burls to carve spoons. The burls gave the wood an interesting pattern of small knots and created a natural curve of the grain in the bowl.

If we couldn't find a burl, we would look for a piece of aspen where a branch stub had been capped over. Aspens are self-pruning and quickly grow over the old dead wood. These would sometimes break into ready-made spoon shapes when we were splitting stovewood, and I always put them aside with the vague intention of making a load of spoons to trade down in Santa Fe.

Other than chopping with a hatchet and carving with gouge or crooked knife, there is not a lot involved in carving spoons (which is why we made them). One of the characters in an 1885 Anton Chekhov story made spoons just to keep busy. "He was trying to make time go faster by getting down to work. His long neck was bent, and he wheezed loudly while he whittled a spoon from a big curved chunk of wood."

But there are other ways to make spoons. Another eastern European mentioned in A. Viires's *Woodworking in Estonia* remembered that the lathe-turned wooden spoons, which became available in about 1900, were much nicer to eat with, but that "old men, who were not used to eating with the factory-made spoons, kept on using homemade spoons for years." After a few years of carving, I too began turning spoons on the lathe. It was faster, and everyone had all the carved ones they could stand. Besides, it was another excuse to work on the lathe.

There's a minor trick to spoon turning. There should be a bend in a spoon where the handle meets the bowl. This is easy to achieve when you carve but requires thought when you turn. The axis of the handle is different from that of the spoon and must be turned in two stages. First, you turn the handle; then you remount the piece and turn the spoon on the axis of the bowl. The second turning obliterates the centering marks of the previous turning. I then saw the face of the bowl and hollow it out with knife and gouge. I enjoy offset spoon turning. It's a miniature version of turning a Queen Anne table leg. Do remember, though, the

[opposite]
The music mill.

[above right]
Turn first on the axis of the handle.

[below right]
Then turn on the axis of the bowl.

[below]
Hollow the bowl with gouge or crooked knife.

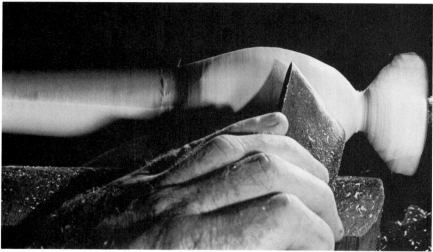

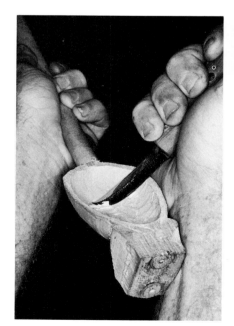

chance of the work flying out of the lathe is greatly enhanced by the out-of-balance load. You could easily end up with a slivered spoon in your mouth.

PIE CRIMPER

Imagine some ancient Babylonian baker rolling out his dough and noticing the repeating pattern left by the nicks and dents in his rolling pin. He adds some deliberate carving to his roller to make his bread a little more decorative than the competition's. His customer who works over at the tax office picks up on the idea and makes an official rolling seal of stone to use on clay documents. Soon the baker is selling more bread and making more profit, which the government is now able to tax equally as fast.

This pie crimper works on the same principle to cut zig-zag strips of dough and trim and seal the edges of pie crust. I turned it from box, but any hard, tight-grained wood will do. The handle is a simple turning job. The cutting wheel is even simpler, just a flat disk, but it does need to be mounted on a mandrel to fit into the lathe. The mandrel is no more than a stick with an X cut on one end for the drive center and a centered cylinder on the other end that is small enough to fit snugly through the wheel's axle hole. When you have split out the blank for the wheel, drill the axle hole, saw around the circumference, mount it on the mandrel and then on the lathe. Turn the disk true with the back edge of the gouge lightly skimming the surface. When the disk is true, turn guidelines for the zig-zags around its perimeter on the edge and on both faces.

When you are clear of the lathe, you can mark the length of the zigs and zags with a pair of dividers. If you set the dividers equal to the thickness of the disk, the angles will be right (90 degrees). Establish a starting point and pace around a few times, resetting as needed to end up with an even number of divisions. Now, on one side of the disk, saw diagonally from the turned guideline on the face to the guideline on the edge at every other point. Do the same thing on the other side to the remaining half of the divider points. The remaining wood can then be removed with a chisel or saw, and then smoothed with a file. Easy.

The handle is a simple bit of spindle turning. Saw both sides of the fork opening and chisel out the end. Make a small shaft of the same wood (thinner in the middle to let the wheel turn freely) and pressure fit it into a hole drilled through both sides of the fork.

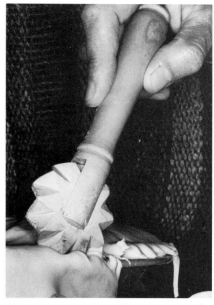

The pie crimper is another turning and carving job.

COLLAPSING CUP

Back in the first century B.C., a Celtic bowl turner was having a bad day. The turned bracelet business wasn't what it used to be. He had to come up with something new—or else it was back to painting himself blue and running around with a battle axe. With the blank already in the lathe and his mead-fueled assistant ready to pull the drive cords, he followed a flash of inspiration and instead of making inwardly curving concentric rings to release a nested set of bowls, he struck straight in with the chisel, producing concentric conic, rather than spherical, sections. Now the turner struck in from the rim to meet the bottom of each of the preceding cuts. As each one fell free, it slid up, only to catch on the top of the one inside of it, which in turn fell free to catch on its interior mate until they were all caught on the others.

The true story of the collapsing cup is lost to history, but my guess that it was a "spin-off" of the technique used to produce "nests of bowls" may not be far off the mark. A. Viires describes their manufacture by traditional woodturners in his *Woodworking in Estonia*. By the late eighteenth century they were being made in silver and called "travelling chalices" in Scotland. Later, in the nineteenth and early twentieth centu-

The outermost ring of the collapsing cup has just been cut free.

ries, they were called "bicycle cups"; many of them were made in tin with a picture of a bicycle embossed on the lid.

A BOX-JOINT DO-NOTHING

Every few years or so an elderly gent (different people, but always of retirement age) will come into the shop, look around at everything with a cursory glance, but eye me cautiously as if sizing me up. When he feels the moment is right, he pulls a small wooden item from his pocket and says, "Got sumpthin' I bet you never seen before." Placing it in my hand he studies my face for the proper reaction as I open and close the tiny pair of box-joint pliers whittled from one piece of wood. "Fantastic!" I say, trying to remember if this is the same man that came in with the same trick two years before. "You keep that," he says "and let me know when you figure *that* one out." He leaves triumphant, and I place the tiny pliers in the drawer with the rest of them, determined someday to do just that.

Here's how you do it. Whittle a 3-inch-long block of soft, even-grained wood such as tulip poplar into a ⅜-inch cross section. Draw a slightly elongated hexagon on two opposing sides about an inch from one end. Draw two more lines connecting the hexagons across each of the two remaining faces. Draw another two lines going with the grain on each of these faces, dividing the space between the two previous lines into three parts, the middle part being equal to half the width of the block.

Now get a very sharp, thin, narrow-bladed knife with the tip sharpened to a chisellike point. Slice outward from the points of the hexagons to the ends of the block. Go as deep as you can, but don't split the block. Now, on each side, cut in on two diagonally opposing angles of the hexagons until you touch the first line on the adjoining faces. Turn to these adjoining faces and get ready for the fun part.

Take the tip end of your knife and push it with a sloping cut across the grain as you see in the picture. Do this on opposite ends of the middle division on either side. These cuts should reach halfway through the block. Now, even more carefully than before, push the knife in with the grain on the two lines, canting the blade back under to cut the area defined by the hexagons.

Go over all of your cuts again to make sure that they connect as they should, and then very slowly pry both ends apart simultaneously. You'll never forget your first time.

Soon you'll be making little wooden pliers by the dozen. They are of no use for holding anything—except your attention—and that only for a very short time. I have a handful of them right now. I guess I'll have to start going around giving them to people.

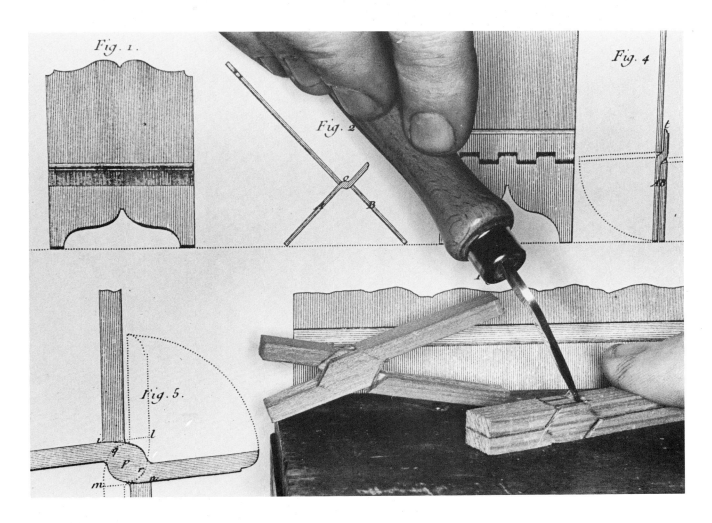

READING STAND

The little pliers have a sophisticated ancestry in the French reading stands.

Slightly more useful than the little pliers, and just as easy to make, is the folding reading stand described by Frenchman Andre Roubo in his *Art of the Cabinetmaker* (1771). As he says, it is *"particulier"* in that, although it hinges open, just like the pliers, it is "one and the same piece." Roubo uses a circular joint (rather than one based on a hexagon). A diamond-shaped joint, like one I found on a recently made example from India, will do just as well and is considerably easier to cut.

Although something that will take as much stress as a reading stand (all those weighty tomes) is best made from walnut, make a few examples in softer wood first to get the idea. I cracked several very nice pieces of walnut before I resorted to elm and cypress to develop my technique.

Even if you had trouble with the pliers, the reading stands will be easy to make. Try the diamond-shaped joint before you attempt the circular one. Draw the diamonds on the sides; the more squashed the diamond, the wider the completed joint will open. Extend three lines that connect the corners of the diamond across the face of the boards, and then divide

The reading stand and the results of
having too much time on your hands.

the width into five or seven equal spaces. Chisel in the alternating
segments until they reach halfway through the plank. Take a rip saw and
cut down the middle of the thickness of the boards until you are square
with the edges of the joint. The spaces between the knuckles of the joint
will have to be made with a coping saw blade inserted through a pre-
drilled hole if you are working in walnut. In soft wood, you can use a
knife, as in the pliers.

One of the wings of Roubo's reading stand is longer than the other to
support the back of the book. Because of this, he thriftily notes that these

reading stands are always made in pairs to keep from wasting wood. By overlapping the two stands as they are cut from the plank with the narrow-bladed French rip bow-saws, nearly a foot of wood can be saved. This is no small consideration when you are using the "beautiful black walnut" (or, as they say in France, "*le beau bois de noyer*").

A RITTENHOUSE HYGROMETER

Not knowing whether you had heard of this instrument, and supposing it would amuse you I have taken the liberty of detailing it to you.
—Thomas Jefferson

To Benjamin Vaughan
Sir   Paris Dec. 29, 1786.
I think Mr. Rittenhouse never published an invention of his in this way, which was a very good one. It was of a hygrometer, which like the common ones was to give the actual moisture of the air. He has two slips of mahogany about 5 I. long, ¾ I. broad and ⅒ I. thick, the one having the grain running lengthwise, and the other crosswise. These are glued together by their faces, so as to form a piece 5 I. long, ¾ I. broad and ⅕ I. thick, which is stuck, by its lower end, into a little plinth of wood thus presenting their edge to the view [fig. 1]. The fibres of the wood you know are dilated but not lengthened by moisture. The slip therefore whose grain is lengthwise, becomes a standard, retaining always the same precise length. That which has its grain crosswise, dilates with moisture and contracts with the want of it. If the right hand piece above represented be the cross grained one, when the air is very moist, it lengthens and forces it's companion to form a kind of interior annulus of a circle on the left thus [fig. 2]. When the air is dry, it contracts, draws its companion to the right, and becomes itself the interior annulus, thus [fig. 3]. In order to shew this dilation and contraction, an index is fixed on the upper end of the two slips; a plate of metal or wood is fastened to the front of the plinth so as to cover the two slips from the eye. A slit, being nearly the portion of a circle, is cut in this plate so that the shank of the index may play freely through its whole range. On the edge of the slit is a graduation, so that the instrument shews somewhat thus [fig. 4]. The objection to this instrument is that it is not fit for comparative observations, because no two pieces of wood being of the same texture exactly, no two will yield exactly alike to the same agent. However it is less objectionable on this account than most of the substances used. Mr. Rittenhouse had a thought of trying ivory: but I do not know whether he executed it. All these substances not only vary from one another at the same time, but from themselves at different times. All of them however have some peculiar advantages, and

Thomas Jefferson's own drawings behind a working copy of the Rittenhouse hygrometer.

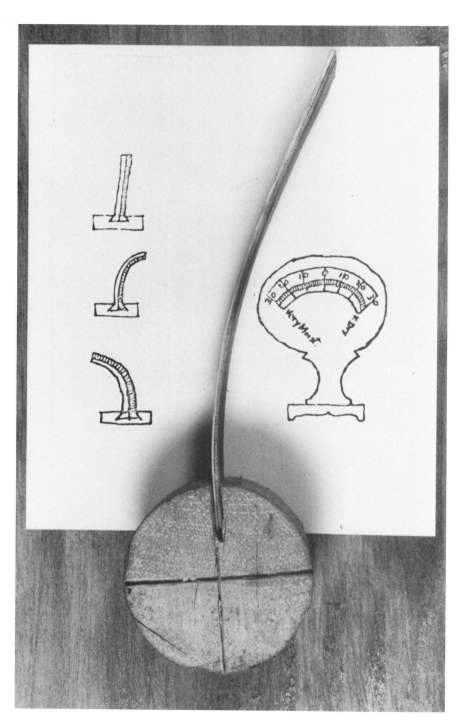

I think this on the whole appeared preferable to any other I had ever seen. I beg you to be assured of the sentiments of perfect esteem and respect with which I have the honor to be Sir your most obedient & most humble servant,

Th: Jefferson

In earlier centuries scientific inquiry was largely a gentlemanly pursuit, undertaken as often by a network of friends as by an institution. David Rittenhouse was a mathematician and astronomer in the times of the Revolution. His interests spanned such extremes as studying the transit of Venus across the face of the sun and the administration of the first United States mint. Rittenhouse was also a woodworker and called a full tool chest left him by his uncle his "great treasure." He was renowned for his scientific instruments—his most famous being his orrery, a working scale model of the solar system.

The instability of wood is usually a nuisance, and so I find it a welcome change to derive some amusement and utility from this property in the hygrometer. I keep mine on the job with me when we are building, using it to indicate when the humidity is low enough to lay flooring that will not shrink apart.

I had seen something like this before. A farmer had a tiny limb nailed to his barn that would move up and down in response to changes in the humidity. How could this branch do what Mr. Rittenhouse had to teach veneer to do? The answer is in the grain. Wood from a branch or from a leaning tree is not the same as that from one that stands straight. In pines and other conifers, the stress of leaning causes the formation of "compression wood." This region of wood with abnormally wide growth rings develops on the underside of the lean.

One characteristic of compression wood is much greater shrinkage along the grain when the wood is seasoned. Normal wood shrinks so little along the length of the grain that the effect is scarcely noticed. In compression wood, however, long-grain shrinkage can be ten times that of normal wood, even reaching as high as 8 percent.

This differential shrinkage, of course, means that a piece that is half compression wood and half normal wood (like a twig) will bend as it dries. Upon reabsorbing water from the air in humid conditions, the piece will tend to return to the position in which it grew. In lumber, we call this interesting principle warping and curse the trouble it causes. In a twig nailed to a barn, we call it a magic weather stick.

LADDER

The best remembered and most often quoted yarn was his claim that in the days of his prime he had made a forty-round ladder in one day and raised it with one hand when finished.
—Walter Rose, *The Village Carpenter*

The first thing that I made when I came to Colonial Williamsburg was almost my last. I arrived six weeks before the rest of the crew and thus was able to devote some time to sharpening the saws and preparing equipment for the jobs to come. It was not the best circumstance to be in, having to borrow both tools and a bench to work at. I spent the first day at

The ladder with the rung pointer and taper auger.

the blacksmith's shop sharpening the 7-foot-long pit saw that we would be using to rip logs into planks for our buildings. The Sheffield steel was almost as trying on the files as the piercing devil-screams of the filing were on the smiths. By mid-morning of the second day they suggested that the wheelwright had a saw-filing vise that might be better suited to my needs.

I worked at the wheelwright's in congenial company—until I cleverly volunteered a brilliant explanation of the art of wheelwrighting to a group of visitors. Among other things, I observed that a wheel was simply a ladder that had been rolled up. I then started in on my version of how to make a wheel. This was far more grating and painful to the sensibilities of men trained in this art than the dullest of files on the sourest of saws. In two days, I was ejected from as many shops. Gradually, I came to understand that filing saws and having brilliant insights into other people's professions are best undertaken in solitude. I decided to begin work on the construction ladders which we would soon be needing.

The wood for the rungs was easy to come by. It was very early spring and there were still plenty of firewood piles about town. As I walked to the shop in the morning light I pulled straight-grained billets of white oak from the frosty piles of lesser stuff. Back at the shop I cut them to length, split them into rough 2 by 2s, shaved them coarsely round, and stacked them log cabin style in the loft to dry.

On the southern coastal plain there is not really any species that is well suited to making the upright sides, or "stiles," of a ladder. Neither the spruce preferred for regular duty nor the proper ash of heavier ladders is to be found. Mark, who was working with Dan the wheelwright, and I went looking for a slow-grown Virginia or shortleaf pine. All the timber that we found either grew too fast in its early years and had a high proportion of weak, short-fibered juvenile wood, or was not straight enough for a ladder. After cutting and rejecting poles from several likely groves, we discovered a patch of proper stuff near a bend in one of the forest roads.

We carried the pole back to the wheelwright's yard (I was not yet allowed back in the shop) and borrowed his felly saw (the pit saw was still not sharpened) to rip it in half down its length. We shaved and roughly trimmed the two pieces, leaving the final smoothing until after the wood had dried.

Three months later, the stuff was dry enough to begin work on. With the stiles side by side, I paced off the 1-foot spaces between the rungs while Mark went over to borrow a tapered bung auger from the coopers. When he returned, I first used the tapered auger to make a hole through a block of 1½-inch-thick oak. This block, with the addition of a blade, became a pencil sharpener–like tool to point the rungs to exactly match the holes that Mark was now boring in the stiles.

With all ready, the rungs (cut to progressively shorter lengths to make the top narrower than the bottom) went into their allotted holes in one of the stiles, which was mounted on the low horses. The top stile had to be worried into place on the score of wriggling rungs until all could be driven together with a mallet and bound with cord. The protruding ends of any of the rungs were planed or drawknifed away.

Now in a small parade we walked the ladder down to the blacksmith's shop to have iron stretchers made which would lock the ladder together. These rods, set beneath selected rungs, keep the whole from coming apart and allow the ladder to give under shock rather than snapping. We have used this ladder for extremely heavy work, and if it endures another decade or two, it might still be around when I am again welcome on the west end of town.

THE CHURN

Dave the cabinetmaker and I were on the way back from looking at a load of upland walnut when the unmistakable form of a 6-foot-diameter great wheel (a human-powered flywheel to drive lathes and the like) jumped out at me from the clutter on the porch of a defunct-gas-station-now-antique-shop.

I convinced Dave to turn around and go back to the shop. As we walked in, I was careful to walk right past the wheel without giving it more than a glance. I knew better than to let the proprietor know where my interest lay. This thing could fetch more than $200, and I was determined not to tip my hand. I said hello to the lady and wandered around looking at this thing and that. Then I saw the churn.

I did not know at first that it was a churn; I thought it was an eggbeater, but it hardly mattered. The action was as clear as it was clever. A wooden frame held two sticks so that one acted as a lever handle to slide the other one back and forth. The horizontal sliding stick was equipped with a leather thong like a bow string that was wrapped around a vertical beater shaft. When the stick slid from side to side, the thong made the beater go round and round.

I forgot all about the wheel. "Dave, come look at this thing!" I shouted.

The lady looked over at me. "This is wonderful!" I said to her. "May I try it?"

"Be my guest," she said.

I worked the lever back and forth, spinning the forked wooden beater and going on about what a significant and charming mechanism it was. I had once shared a garret with a Canadian girl whose father had been a socialist revolutionary dentist and part-time hand-cranked eggbeater designer. She had inherited a steamer trunk full of his inventions—the work of a lifetime—and I spent many a contented hour marveling through the convoluted chromium multitude.

"How much is this? I have got to have it," I cried.

"Well, let me see," she said, barely able to contain herself, "it's on consignment." She went over to the register and looked in a notebook.

"He wants one hundred and twenty dollars. Firm."

I looked at her, then at Dave, then at the seven little pieces of nailed together wood. There was no way that it was going home with me. I thanked the lady and giving a last sad look at the beater, I headed out the door. I was halfway down the steps when I remembered the great wheel.

"What do you want for the wheel?" I asked the disappointed lady.

"That thing? Oh . . . ten dollars."

I paid cash.

My copy of the elusive churn.

SWIFT

Swifts are skein holders. When the spinner has spun all that she can spin, she winds her yarn onto a niddy noddy to form an open skein for dyeing. After the skein is dry, the swift, expanding within it like an umbrella, will hold it for rewinding onto shuttle bobbins for weaving. Like spinning wheels, swifts occasionally served a more symbolic than utilitarian role in upper-class households. These icons of domesticity were often turned and carved of whale or elephant ivory. Far more significant to me are the real tools made for real work.

Swifts are usually lathe turned and equipped with threaded set screws. Of all the swifts that I have seen, a simple carved one without any turning at all is my favorite. It mounts on the edge of the table with a wedge such as you might use on a marking gauge. Instead of the bottom hub sliding up to expand the swift, the top hub drops down and is held down by pins placed through holes in the shaft.

A swift is a simple enough thing to make: see one—make one. The hubs can be turned on a mandrel similar to that used to make the wheel for the pie crimper. The only joints are made with string; so if you can tie a knot, you can put one together. The thin sticks of the swift can be shaped any number of ways. I split them out of hickory and plane them smooth, temporarily setting them in a shallow groove in an oak board to guide the planing to a consistent thickness.

A SIX-BOARD CHEST

Everybody likes the six-board chest. These boxes (literally) carry a lot of cultural baggage. True tales are told of how that chest at the foot of the bed once held all the possessions of the family on the trip from the Old World.

The long sides are just great wide boards. The only joinery is dado and rabbet work fastened with nails. You may not see the point of the rabbeting, as it adds little to the strength of the chest. The rabbets are essential, though, to make the chest tight against dirt and vermin. Simple butting is about as effective in sealing out the elements as a door without a stop around the jambs.

Start with the sides. Plane the rabbets around the bottoms and the ends. When you go with the grain you will have little difficulty; across the grain, be sure that the edge of the rabbet is nipped with a knife before the plane passes. Many fancy rabbet planes, called moving fillisters, have little knives inset just ahead of the blade. Lacking one of these special planes, you can use a cutting gauge or a knife and a straightedge.

Cutting the housings for the till (the little box in the upper corner) is more involved than cutting the sides, because it is partially enclosed rather than open-ended. Start either by boring an auger hole or by chiseling a shallow mortice at the intersection of the two grooves. The

[opposite]
The swift, made with only a whittling knife (collection of Colonial Williamsburg).

Six-board chest.

groove that runs with the grain can be cut by sawing from the outside edge to this landlocked hollow and then chiseling out the wood between the two kerfs. The cross-grain stopped dado can be cut only by scoring both sides with a knife prior to chiseling.

The lid for the till pivots on dowels carved onto or inset into its back corners. These dowels turn in shallow holes bored into the side boards of the chest. The open lid of the till serves as a prop to hold the lid of the chest open.

The two end boards of this chest extend below the width of the sides to form the legs. They are shaped on their underside in the form of two ogee curves converging into an arch. The ogees are easy to generate with

Cut a dado in the end board for the bottom.

a compass and a straightedge, and just as easily cut out with a narrow-bladed bow saw. The edges of the end boards need to be cut away to enable the side boards to sit flush with the feet. Across the inside of the end boards, you will need to cut a dado to house the end of the bottom. You can make two saw kerfs and chisel out the waste, or use a special dado plane. Dado planes are made in varying widths, and are adjustable only in respect to the depth to which they cut. Since it has no fence, the dado plane must run against a board clamped or nailed to the work.

This chest appears to violate one of the laws of the dynamics of wood. How can the cross grain of the sides be fastened to the long grain of the ends without the problems of differential swelling and shrinking? Such crossing of the grain in this chest would seem to have the makings of a self-destructing four-cornered Rittenhouse hygrometer. The answer is in the weakness of the fasteners. The nails that hold the sides are able to crush and flex in the fibers of the wood and allow for a great deal of movement. If we used pegs or some other unyielding fastening, the boards would split apart.

An applied moulding surrounds the base of the chest. You make this moulding by planing it onto the edge of a board and then sawing it off. The miters in the corners should be cut in a miter box. As always, position the moulding in the miter box so that the teeth of the saw cut into the face side of the moulding. Like a bullet, a saw makes a bigger mess where it leaves an object than where it enters.

MUSIC MILL

You may think I dreamed this one up, but somewhere in the Swiss Alps there is a little water wheel turning a cogged cylinder to lift and drop tiny trip-hammers on wine bottles and play what might loosely be termed

Housings for the till and the pivot for the lid.

music. Typically Swiss, it works the same way as a music box. I know that it's true—I saw it in a National Geographic film when I was eleven.

There are two ends to this machine: the cylinder end where the work goes in and the bottle end where the sound comes out. In any design problem one must first consider the factors that cannot be changed. In this music mill it is the width of the bottles; without getting complicated (for example, arranging the bottles in staggered tiers) you can not place

An instrument anyone can play.

the average wine bottle closer than on 4-inch centers. Decide how many notes you want the mill to be able to play (six is a good start) and that is how wide the bottle end of the trip-hammers will need to be.

If you begin with the cogged cylinder that records the music, be sure to give it sufficient length and circumference for all the notes that you want to play. About 10 inches long and 5 inches in diameter will do for basic classical themes. I used a small log of tulip poplar that seemed about the right size and turned it down on the lathe to a proper cylinder. You will have to stay with whatever size that you begin with when you make a new cylinder to play another tune. While the cylinder was still in the lathe, I scored it with dividers at 1-inch intervals to indicate the spacing for the cogs. This gave the hammer levers enough room to clear each other without their having to be made overly small. When the turning is done, bore holes to accept the 1-inch-diameter axles on each end of the cylinder.

Music in its crudest form (what we have here) is simply a sequence of notes, each with its specific pitch and duration. In order to record your music, you must first reduce it to this level. On a sheet of paper, lay out vertical lines an inch apart for each of the different notes. If you arrange the bottles in the typical fashion with the low notes on the left ascending to the right, then the left-most line represents the lowest note of the music, moving on up to the highest on the right. Label the lines with their notes and begin at the bottom of the page. Mark the first note with an X and then measure up the appropriate distance to the next note, 1 inch for a whole note, ½ inch for a half note, and so on. Locate the pitch of the next note and mark it, continuing until the end. Graph paper makes this a lot easier.

When you have it all down on paper, wrap it around the cylinder and poke through the Xs to transfer the marks to the wood. I made one cylinder from a scrap beech log. I knew that it would crack open or "check," as whole stem wood is prone to do. Such a cylinder should actually be made from a section split from one side of the heart of a tree twice as large. But the little log was what I had and it remained intact until I left it near the fire one night. The next day there was a ¾-inch-wide radial crack in the cylinder. Fortunately the spirit of the music was in favor with the spirit of the wood and the crack appeared harmlessly between the beginning and the end of the tune. Music hath charms to soothe the salvage beech.

At each spot marked for a note, bore a quarter-inch hole, say ⅜ inch deep, into the cylinder. Into each of these holes drive an inch-long wooden pin. The depth of the holes and the length of the pins must be consistent. Otherwise the timing will be thrown off. Don't glue the pegs; you may want to adjust them or even rebore the cylinder for a new set of pegs and a whole new tune. I am working on a cylinder that plays the theme from "Swan Lake" and then can be shifted to the side so that an alternate set of pegs will play "Under My Thumb."

The trip-hammers work like overbalanced see-saws. Pushing down on one end raises the other. When the cog slips off the end and releases it, the other end comes swinging down and strikes the bottle. The shafts of the hammers are ¾ inch wide and taper in their length down to the hammer head. The hammers are 3-inch-long pieces of hardwood, slotted to fit on the ends of the shafts.

Because the cylinder with the pegs is much narrower than the array of bottles, the hammer shafts will need to fan out. They need to be separated by spacers that will also hold their ¼-inch axle rod. The surest way to hold these spacers is to inset them into a board. Lay out the shafts so that they cross a 3-inch-wide board set 18 inches from the hammer ends. See that they are evenly spaced so as to hit the bottles at one end and the proper cogs at the other. Take a scratch awl and mark the spaces between them on the board.

Now make enough identical spacers to fit between all of the hammers and the ends. Bore through these in the same location to allow passage of the axle rod. Now set the spacers on the spaces marked between the hammers and slide them all a little forward so that the space between them increases enough to give the hammer shafts clearance to swing freely. Mark along their sides and saw down ¼ inch on these lines. Chisel the wood out to make tapered slots to hold the spacer blocks. Bore ¼-inch holes through the hammer shafts, enlarging them enough to allow them to pivot freely on the axle rod. Assemble the alternating hammer shafts and spacers on the long axle rod and drive the spacers into their slots in the board. You could also nail the spacers between two boards but I believe the tapered slots are just as easy (though harder to explain).

Build the hammer array and the cylinder into a frame to hold them in the proper arrangement. Saw the ends of the hammers off in an even line so that they will engage the cogs on the cylinder equally.

You must mount the bottles so that they will ring when you strike them. Anything that touches the sides of the bottles has the potential to damp the sound. The best method of suspension, then, would be to hang them on a string by their necks, but it would be difficult for the gravity hammers to strike them without some additional linkage. The most successful arrangement I have found is to catch the bottleneck into a hole just slightly larger than itself. Thus suspended, the bottles are neatly held with minimum interference with the sound.

Bottles ring like bells when you strike them and, true enough, cheap bottles sound like cheap bells. If you find that the tone is short and clunky, the glass is probably too thin. I recommend a Mouton Cadet or any of the '76 Burgundies. Once you have the bottles you will of course need to tune them. The more liquid there is in the bottle, the lower the tone. Set the bottles in their rack and start with the highest note, alternately filling and striking it until it rings true. Tune the next bottle and continue until they all sound right. If you are starting with full wine bottles, begin with the lowest note and drink just enough to set it right. Go to the next highest and drink it down to tune it up. You should be hearing beautiful music by the time you finish.

8 ROWBOAT

"Yes, I'm very fond of boats myself. I like the way they're—contained. You don't have to worry about which way to go, or whether to go at all—the question doesn't arise, because you're on a boat, aren't you?"

—Tom Stoppard, *Rosencrantz and Guildenstern Are Dead*, 1967

I like this design for the first-time boatbuilder. It is only 8 feet long and easy enough, and yet it involves many of the techniques of more complex work. It is a few steps above the "carpenter's boat," which is no more than a waterproof box. As in any real boat, you must measure and cut bevel joints, but only a few. The snub bow makes for easier bends than a pointed stem would require. The flat bottom is a simple version of carvel (butted and caulked) boatbuilding. You build up the sides from two overlapping planks and rivet them together as you do in a lapstrake boat.

This is a little boat. I use it to tow logs that I have cut in the hills back down the river to the shop. It moves very fast with one adult in it, but gets mighty sluggish and low in the water when loaded with much over two hundred pounds. Still, my daughters and I have rowed many a mile back and forth across the river when the bridge at the mill dam is washed out.

I started building this design of boat when I was twelve. It was an adventure then, but even now I appreciate how the search for the arcane necessities of the boatbuilder's trade can send me down some unfamiliar paths. Where do you find things like cotton for caulking the seams?

THE BOATYARD

"You want to go to K. T. Smith's railway down in Dare," said the man who sold me the copper nails. "He's got caulking cotton. He's got a log boat down there too."

I found the way to Dare on a truckstop map above the naughty books. I turned onto Railway Road, which led from the highway right down to the water. I rolled down the narrow, whipping lane where the green trees brushed the windows of the truck. I steered quick turns around ripe fenced gardens and emerald cow pastures. The sign came up on the left.

K. T. Smith's
Marine Railway
1842

There were none of the signs of a business—just a well-kept old farmhouse with white painted outbuildings along the water. One of the buildings at the end of the lane sported a faded and rusting blue disk stating the presence of a pay phone.

I pulled off the lane beside a narrow gate. No one seemed to be around. Off in the water I could see what must have been the log boat. It was much bigger than I had expected, gleaming white like the buildings. I walked in under the walnuts and hackberries. A smoldering mound of planer chips twisted the air with preservative vapor. I walked past the first building to what was obviously the railway, a sort of trolley arrangement sloping down into the water to pull boats up to where they could be cleaned and repaired. The winches were rusty, but not to the extent of abandoned equipment.

The boat with a hull of sculpted logs.

The boatyard on a busy day.

The tin-covered shed to the right was cluttered with boat lumber. Inside one wing I could see a belt-driven drill press and a hand-driven post drill. A workbench on the left wall was covered with strips of rubber and trash, but from the exotic contours of its planks I could see it had once been dapper. A small sawmill was embedded in the wood-dirt in front of the shed. It was in the same shape as the railway—unused but usable. Nearby, a barn held a half dozen horse collars and rotted harness. A cart stood nearby loaded with a sad saddle and cardboard boxes. There was no horse. Returning to the railway, still looking for the owners, I found the huge belt-driven power planer sitting by its end. There was also a rusting homemade iron-wheeled log cart. This had been a busy boatyard in its day.

I walked back to the road to see if I could find someone. Three men were working in the garden beyond a row of great pecan trees at the turn in the lane. They were loading wooden crates of potatoes into a cart slowly pulled by an old red tractor. They saw me approaching but did not stop working. I called out once to them, but apparently not loud enough to make them stop. I called out again and they stopped at the next box. The look of the men told me that any moron would have known to wait until they reached the end of the row. I told them I was looking for the Mr. Smith who runs the boatyard.

"I'm him."

"Randy Wilson told me I could get cotton from you. I need some cotton for corking" (I hoped I said it right) "the bottom of a rowboat."

The old man told the youngest man to go help me out. We walked through the gate (a rural classic, strong and light) to the first building. He unlocked the door; it was the storehouse. Inside were a dozen kegs of copper and galvanized nails. Cans of paint lined the walls. The cotton was in a box behind one of two counters that bounded the aisle down the middle. There was a dusty pay phone on the wall.

"How much do you want?"

"Well, enough for a rowboat," I answered.

He looked out the window for a moment and then placed a large paper-wrapped hank on the counter.

"I need some seam compound too," I said.

"How much?"

"Well, enough for a rowboat."

He placed a single can on the counter.

"Need some paint too," I said.

He looked out the window again. "Enough for a rowboat?"

"Yeah."

"Need anything else?"

"Do you have any inch and a half copper nails?"

"No, I got some Monel."

"No, I want to do this all the old way."

I saw him look at me for the first time, but only for an instant. "That all?"

"Yes."

He began to total. Beside me in the corner there leaned a two-man crosscut saw. It was sharp and well oiled, the metal a deep sable.

"This your family business?" I asked. He looked up, but not at me. He was pleasant enough, but I was a stranger at an inconvenient time. I wondered for a moment if he were blind, but the figuring he was doing made that unlikely. "Yes, that man is my father."

"How long has this been in your family?"

"Since 1842."

I saw some ledger books on the top of one of the shelves. I pointed to the stacks of pale blue volumes on top of the shelves. "And those are the old ledgers?"

"Some of them. The really old ones are up in the attic."

I paid him forty dollars and leaned out the door as he made some more notes in his ledger.

"That a log boat out there?" I asked. I had never seen one of those sculpted vessels before.

"Yeah, that's one of 'em. There's another one down at the end of the dock. The other one was built here. It's not in such good a shape as that."

"Can I walk out and look at it? I won't fall in."

"Go ahead."

I set my cans and cotton in the grass beside the store and walked down to the pier. The water was full of minnows, white drifting jellyfish, and jumping mullet. Across the wide creek (as they are called locally) dull green cedars stood like giant chessmen. The two boats were brilliantly painted many times over. The iron work was hand forged. The boats were damp and oily in the holds where I studied the marks left by adzes in the years of prohibition. The stern was bounded by a prim gallery of turned posts. The boat was surprisingly narrow. It looked like the house.

I walked up through the boatyard. The boxes of potatoes were now in the back of a truck driven by the older man. He looked at me.

"Hot this morning, isn't it?" he said.

"Sure is. Get all your potatoes in?"

He didn't answer.

WOOD

Back in town, I went to buy my wood—heart cypress resawn from old building timbers. Eastern white cedar, or juniper, as it is usually called, is the prime material for small boats. Western red, Alaska, and Port Orford cedars are also good. As these may be hard to find away from the coast, white pine, spruce, or even yellow pine will do. You want stock that is as clear and straight-grained as possible; but small knots that can be filled with plugs are acceptable. I use cypress because I can get it. Like white pine, it tends to absorb a lot of water (but doesn't rot), making for a heavier boat. Even so, one strong person can carry this little boat.

The wood determines the form of the boat in more than its length, breadth, and thickness. The flex of the wood determines the curvature and lines of the boat. For a boat to have good lines you must select long side planks that are as similar as possible to place in opposing positions on the boat. They must bend evenly to give proper shape to the boat.

The stem and transom need to be as stout as the sides are supple. Pine boards 1½ inches thick are best, but if you can't find such thick wood, you can use thinner stock and add a batten to the sides and bottom. You

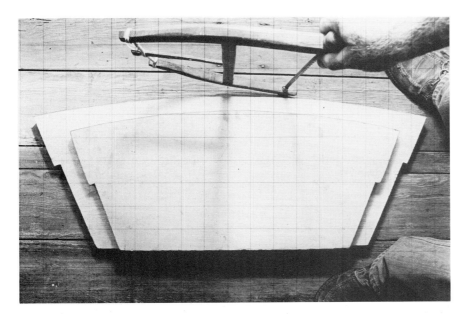

The stem on the transom (grid on 2-inch squares).

Nail on the building boards.

will have to do the same thing to the lower edge of the thin side planks to enable you to nail on the bottom boards.

Start with the stem and transom. Saw them to the indicated outline and plane their faces smooth. Their edges, square now, will need to be beveled parallel with the angle of the curving side planks. These angles will have to be determined by trial assembly. Boats are "collections of curves and angles" that you cannot predict until the pieces are in place.

Before you can bend the sides, though, the stem and transom need to be fastened in position with building boards. Stand the stem and transom

8 feet apart; span the distance with a scrap board and nail it down. Turn this assemblage over, pull in the bottom edges until they are 7 feet 6 inches apart and nail another board to them. Adjust the tilt of the stem until it leans back 4 inches out of plumb. This is the angle that makes the bow ride over the mighty waves. Check that the stem and transom are parallel by measuring for equal diagonals from corner to corner. Since they will want to fall over, put in an angled block or nail on a diagonal support.

(Because you build this boat mostly upside down, the terms upper and lower can be confusing. I will refer to the side planks by their nautical names: the garboard plank is the one closest to the bottom of the sea; the sheer plank, closest to the sky.)

Cut the 10-foot-long, ½-inch-thick stock for the side planks close to their final widths: 10 inches wide for the garboard, 7 inches for the sheer. They may spring unevenly or split if you saw off a lot of wood after they are bent.

(Take care with this bending. I remember during my adolescent boat-building career trying to bend the planks into a pointed-bow sailboat. I was working behind the house in an area illuminated by the alley light and fireflies. The planks were 1-by-12-inch pine boards liberated from the attic floor. I poured pans of boiling water down the heavy planks and pulled them together on the transom with a twisted rope windlass. Suddenly the screws pulled out of the stem and the boat exploded. Two steaming planks flew across the yard at kneecap level. One cartwheeled the serving table at a patio party my mother was having for the neighbors. The other demolished a flower garden. I ran.)

Take the two 10-inch-wide planks that will form the sides and set them spanning the shoulders of the stem and transom. These are the garboard planks. Loop stout cords around the ends with knots that can be readily tightened. Now cut a spreader stick 36 inches long that will determine the width, or "beam," of the boat. This spreader will bend out the side planks to allow you to measure the angles that you will have to cut on the edges of the stem and transom. To prevent slipping, it may be necessary to drive a small, snipped-off nail into each end of this spreader to make points that will bite into the wood. Inset this stick amidships, pull the loops tight, and recheck the stem and transom to see that they are parallel. You can see the angle that you need now; all you have to do is record it and cut it.

You can record the angle with a bevel, as most boatbuilders do, or with dividers, setting them to the width of the gap on the inside of the corner formed by the sides and the ends, and then transferring and scribing this measurement on the outside. In any event, the measured gap or the bevel angle should be equal on both sides of the stem and transom.

The drawknife and the slick are two tools well suited to shaping these angles on the end grain of the stem and transom. They can reach right up to the shoulder. Work with the ends still nailed in their frame. When the

Draw in the garboard planks.

[left]
Measure the angle of intersection at each end.

[right]
Cut the measured bevels onto stem and transom.

bevels look right, set the boards and their stretcher back in place and see that they are indeed tight both inside and out.

Now you can put the sides and stretcher on for the last time. Waterproof the joint by coating it with marine glue or paint before assembly. Fasten the planks to stem and transom with 1¼-inch brass screws. Use one screw every 2 inches or so. Be sure to drill pilot holes for all fasteners. You can save a little money by using screws only on the edges and nailing in between. See that the joint is flat and true before you screw. If you try to use the screws to pull the joints together, you may split the boards.

The boat is now ready for the sheer planks. Lay them around the garboard planks and pull them in with the cords as before. The two should overlap 1½ inches on their sides. Make any trimming on the sheer planks, not the garboard. Again, measure the angle needed at the stem and stern, take the boards off and shave the bevels as before. In this case, since you do not have to go up to a shoulder, you can use a common

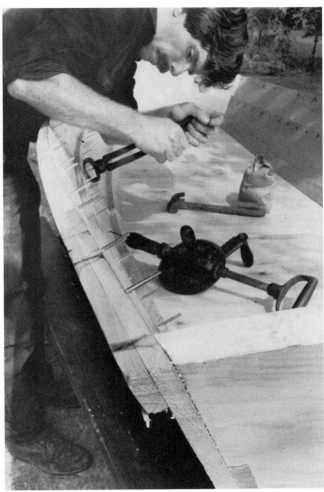

plane (you could have used one before if you had a bullnose plane). Fasten the ends down as before.

RIVETING

The two side planks overlap each other by 1½ inches; therefore, the centerline of this seam will be ¾ inch from either edge. Run your rivets along this line, one every 3 inches. Predrill the holes for the rivets; you don't want to run the risk of splitting the planks and ruining the work. I use copper nails and washers rather than regular boat nails and proper "roves" because I had them. (One mail-order source for nails and roves is the Tremont Nail Company, Box 111, Wareham, Mass. 02571.)

Drive the nail through from the outside until the head crushes slightly into the wood. Place a rove around the nail and tap it tight against the wood on the inside with a hollow punch, "rove iron," or "burr starter," a

[left]
Flex a batten to give you the lines.

[right]
Join the sides with nails, snipped off and then riveted over washers.

Shave the chines, the garboard planks, and the stem and transom into the same plane so that the bottom can be nailed on.

stout iron or brass cylinder with a ⅜-inch hole in it. Snip the nail off less than ⅛ inch, or a distance equal to one and a half times the diameter of the nail, above the rove. Back up the outside with a heavy hammer or an old flat iron as you peen the inside over with tapping from a light riveting hammer. Do not cut the nail too long or use too heavy a hammer—the nail may bend in the wood and cause a split. Tap light to draw tight.

You will enjoy riveting; the bapping of the hammer makes the copper flow into a satisfying mushroom head. The tone of the tapping goes up as the rivet is set. On this little boat with one line of rivets, there is not so much that you tire of it, and although you could do it all yourself, it gives you a legitimate cause to request some company holding the backing iron.

Now that the planks are joined, you can dispense with the stretcher bar after making and fitting a seat amidships. It should be 36 inches at its longest point. Fasten it to battens set beneath each end held in place with carefully placed screws. It should be stiff enough that it does not flex excessively under your weight and damage the planks. The bow and stern seats will need similar custom fitting, but be sure that angles that should be equal, are.

LINES

So far, the garboard and sheer planks have been left just as they were in the lumber stack. They hang over the edges of the stem and transom. The planks need to be shaped so that they are wider amidships than they are at either end, that is, curved rather than straight from end to end. Just as the flex of the planks gave the lines of the boat in one plane, the flex of a specially made wooden batten will guide the lines from stem to stern. This batten is a strip ½ inch square selected for even grain and uniform bending.

It does not matter if you set and cut the trim lines on the garboard or sheer planks first, but do both of one or the other at a time so that they will be as similar as possible. The procedure is the same for both. Take a small clamp and fasten one end of the batten level with the corner of the stem. Place a small nail amidships in the sheer plank 5½ inches above the line of rivets. Bend the batten over this and clamp the free end at the corner of the transom. Reset the clamp on the stem end to be sure that it is not torquing the batten away from its natural curve. When you are sure that you like the curve, trace it on the plank. Repeat the process on the opposite sheer plank. The procedure on the garboard plank is the same, the middle nail placed 8 inches from the bottom line of rivets.

When both sides are lined out, you can shave or rip saw away the excess wood. Be very careful if you saw, cutting well onto the waste side of the line. Be sure that nothing twists or pulls on the waste piece that might cause it to split away. On the sheer plank, take a long plane and smooth the lines from end to end, blending them into the stem and transom. Trim the bottoms of the stem and transom to match. More leveling will have to be done after the chine is installed.

Saw off the bottom boards even with the planks.

THE CHINE

The 1 by 2 inch chine supports the intersection of the garboard plank and the bottom boards. It is a pretty stiff piece (white oak would be good here if you are short of other stock) and will need to soaked or steamed before it can be bent into place. The simplest method to limber up such a long piece of wood is to wrap it in damp rags and pour boiling water on it. Cut one end to a tight fit against the transom, clamp it along the length of the plank and eyeball the other end to cut it to a proper seat against the inside of the stem. Work from the inside of the boat, cutting off more and more as needed. Fasten it with screws from the outside spaced every 6 inches.

The boards for the bottom (¾ by 6 inch stock) need to be fitted onto a flat surface, which means that the canted bottom edges of the chine and garboard plank must be planed smooth. Take one of the bottom boards and use it as a straight edge to span the bottom to guide the planing. When you have the bottom flat, go around the outside again, planing in a

Seagull's eye view, with a six-inch grid superimposed.

caulking bevel. This is a secondary bevel on the outer edge to allow you to stuff in cotton and seam compound. The gap on the outside should be ⅛ inch wide and tapered to nothing at a depth of ½ inch. Don't neglect the stem and transom bevels.

The boards for the bottom need not only a bevel but an actual gap between them. As they absorb water, they will of course swell; if they are forced together too tightly, they will buckle and pull loose. Plane the edges of the bottom boards so that they are ¹⁄₁₆ inch out of square. Drill pilot holes for the nails, and drive them in, three to a board. Space each board ¹⁄₁₆ inch from its neighbor. When all the boards are on, saw their ends flush with the sides and plane them smooth.

The final parts are the keelson (a keel would be on the outside) and the bow and stern seats. The ½-inch-thick, 5-inch-wide keelson must be nailed down the middle, the nails clinched across the grain of the bottom boards. When it is in place, the seats can be fitted and fastened. Rivet a 1½-inch-wide rubrail along the rim of the sheer plank to protect

Push cotton into the bevels and fill the remainder of the gap with seam compound. Caulk between bottom boards and garboard plank as well.

"Art is all of a boat but the wood."
Thoreau

it and turn back a few splashes. Use the same ½-inch stock and rivet or clench nail it every 4 inches.

The only ribs in this boat double as the mounts for the oarlocks. These tapered oak 2 by 4s reach from the chines to 3 inches above the rubrails. Fasten them with brass screws from the outside.

Now for the caulking. Sand the boat all over, taking care to go with the grain of the wood. Now give the boat its first coat of paint or varnish (it's up to you, but I want my wood to be seen). Be sure to coat inside all of the seams that you intend to caulk. When the finish is dry, take a putty knife and push cotton hand tight along the gaps. Push too hard and you will shove it right out the other side. Fill in on top of the cotton with seam compound. When it has set up, give the boat another thorough sanding and another coat of paint or varnish. One more sanding and brushing will make three coats, which is the bare minimum. Paint the name on the transom.

Don't be surprised at leaks when you first put your boat in the water. Just as in a wooden bucket, the wood needs to swell up to be tight. Buy a large sponge before you go out. If you want, you can put sodden sacks on the overturned boat to swell up the wood before you take it down to the water. Even so, you will still take in a little water. In no case should you drill holes in the bottom of your boat to let the water out.

9

A FIELD GUIDE
TO AMERICAN
TOOL MARKS

"Excellent!" I cried.
"Elementary," said he.

—Sir Arthur Conan Doyle, *The Memoirs of Sherlock Holmes*

WHENEVER we get to talking about woodcutting, the story of the aspen tree is sure to come up. Our mountain valley had been host to the first wave of the back-to-the-landers of the late 1960s. One day when Terry was walking near one of their abandoned campsites beside the creek, he saw an aspen tree that someone had half-heartedly attempted to fell, first with an axe, and then with a wavering bucksaw. Both of these attempts had been abandoned less than a third of the way through the tree. The aspen had been felled, however, and was lying across the pond. Just above the weathered gray axe and saw cuts, the tree had been freshly severed by the paired chisel teeth of a beaver.

Tool traces tell stories. They can tell the careful detective when a job was done, how it was done, and something about the person who did it. Reading the strokes of an axe, the angles of gougings, the pattern of chisel cuts, is a way to learn from teachers long dead.

The traces of the tools are also valuable to those concerned primarily with the object itself. Because the dates of invention of some tools are known, tool marks can often be used to date artifacts. For example, a chest that shows the marks of a circular saw on it could not have been made before about 1800, when the circular saw came into use.

The reverse of this method of dating, however, does not hold true. Although we can be reasonably sure about the beginning date of a given technique, the past is always with us. Anyone can pick up an old spoon bit auger and leave marks that are indistinguishable from those of five centuries earlier. This is the stock-in-trade of the antiques faker.

But the problem is not just that of deliberate deception. New techniques will be adopted only when they fit into the cultural and economic environment of a region. Just as in dendrochronology, in which the variations in annual tree ring widths caused by changes in the local climate are used as a dating tool, dating by tool marks must take into account the particular history of the area. Archaic tools and techniques may endure in one locality long after they have been replaced by newer methods elsewhere. Labor, capital, material resources, markets, transportation, and cultural preferences all have their influence. Only with a thorough knowledge of local history can one evaluate the significance of a given clue.

Juggling. Regularly spaced notches running across the grain of hewn timbers are indicative of a process known in some areas as "juggling." Hewers square round logs by splitting off segments between notches cut every foot or so along the length of the log. These notches are often removed by subsequent working of the timber. The notches may appear to center on large knots in the timber. Because chunks cannot be split free if they contain large knots, the notches must be spaced to remove them.

[above]
Squaring a log by "juggling"—notching and splitting off chunks.

[below]
The two deep notches in the timber over this doorway are evidence of the hewer's technique.

[opposite]
These pit saw marks on an oak timber halt abruptly at an embedded piece of barbed wire. Ergo, the sawing must have been done after the invention of barbed wire.

[above]
The hewer follows his splitting by cross-grained slicing with the broad axe.

[right]
Marks of the broad axe cover this Hyde County, North Carolina, timber.

Broad axe. The diagonal or transverse sweep of the broad axe is valuable in identifying the work of a single hewer and his axe on separate structures. Both the tool and the user leave distinctive patterns on the timber. The stop marks of the axe record the contour of the blade along with any nicks in its edge. It is tempting to try to assign chronological or ethnic categories to broad axe blade forms, but the range of patterns is too diverse for safe generalizations.

Carpenter's adze. The adze, like the axe, dates to antiquity. Its marks are not a reliable means of dating materials, but they do show the characteristic technique of the individual craftsman. Like the broad axe, the adze is commonly used diagonally, or across the grain of the wood. In skilled hands it produces an exceptionally smooth surface. Cross-grained axe or adze work done on dry timber often shows more torn wood fibers than that done on green timber.

Lipped shipwright's adze. The lipped shipwright's adze is designed to cut deep channels across the grain in ship timbers. The lips on either side of the blade sever the grain to prevent splintering. Early surfaces cut with a lipped adze are rare outside of marine work. Although these tools may be quite ancient, I have not found them listed in catalogs before the mid-nineteenth century.

Concave hollowing. Short, smooth hollows within a concave surface indicate bowl adze work. The same process done with a gouge and mallet often shows longer hollows and the evidence of individual blows of the mallet. Concave work smoothed by a curved pull-knife or scorp can often be detected by "chatter," tiny lines perpendicular to the line of passage of the tool caused by vibration.

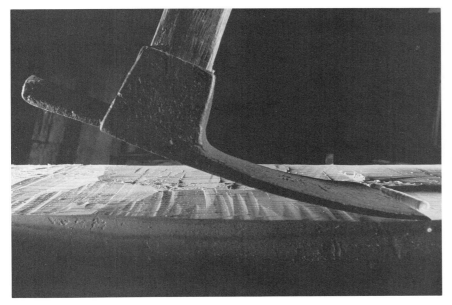

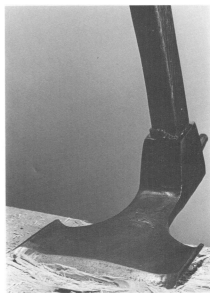

[above left]
Adzing along the grain leaves a smooth, undulating surface.

[below left]
The marks on this bowl were made by a gouge, rather than by a scorp, like the one in the foreground. The chattermarks of a scorp are shallower and closer together.

[above right]
The lipped shipwright's adze is particularly suited to cross-grained work.

[below right]
The end of this poplar-log feeding trough was shaped with an axe. The interference of the axe handle forced the shift in blade angle seen in the lower corners.

The peg at the upper left was probably chiseled to a point a few inches from its hole. The carpenter who worked on this North Carolina barn was standing off to the lower left or upper right.

Chisel and hatchet stops. The marks left on a surface used as a chopping block are often associated with peg shaping. They are often found in concealed places on furniture, such as near the peg used as a stop for the extendable supports of a drop-front desk. Chisel marks are usually found in close proximity to the actual peg hole, as the work was done by eye to a custom fit. Extensive cross-hatching on a timber may indicate that it was facing up during the construction process, a potential clue in determining the order of assembly.

Corner chisel or bruzz. Look for contiguous stop marks across the corners of a mortice. This tool seems to have an earlier association with wheelwrights than with carpenters. Diderot's 1763 *Encylopédie* identifies it as a carpenter's or wheelwright's tool, but Joseph Smith's 1816 *Key to Sheffield Manufactories* calls it a wheeler's chisel. The 1890 Buck Brothers tool catalog, however, lists five sizes, from ¾ to to 1¼ inches, but makes no mention of wheelwrights. Morticing in normal construction wood with a common chisel relies partially on long grain splitting, a process that is not as effective in the unsplittable elm wood of wheel hubs. Thus, wheelwrights often use augers followed by corner chisels that can square the round hole by simultaneously slicing both the end grain and the interlocked long grain. Use by carpenters appears less frequently, and generally not until late in the nineteenth century.

Gouge. Scribed joints such as those found in window sash can be made with either planes or gouges, but only the gouge can undercut the middle, making it slightly bowl-shaped. Subtle deviations from the straight line are often the only way to distinguish gouge-work from planing in joinery and cabinetwork. When other evidence is lacking, the presence of gouge marks around an auger hole may indicate the use of a nose auger, which requires a gouge-cut depression to allow the auger to start cutting.

Spoon bit. The spoon bit gained a certain notoriety recently in the case of a famous antique forgery. A supposed seventeenth-century Brewster chair in a large museum was proved to be a modern fake when it was shown that its creator used a spiral auger (a much later innovation) rather than a spoon bit. The round-bottomed profile of the spoon bit is easily distinguished from the square end of the spiral auger. The use of a spoon bit is no proof of age, however; it is still preferred by chairmakers.

Corner chisels leave contiguous lines across the inside corners of mortices.

Nose auger. The nose or shell auger came soon after the spoon bit. Both forms are needed, but the nose auger is better suited for the larger holes of carpentry. The nose auger is shown in Moxon's 1687 *Mechanick Exercises* and is common in carpentry work throughout the eighteenth

[above left]
The interior of this gouge rack was shaped by the same tools that it protects.

[above right]
The spoon bit.

[left]
The shell, nose, or pod auger lacks a lead screw, but has a sharpened blade which acts as a rotary chisel. The end grain is usually left rather ragged by this auger.

Three auger bit holes show their characteristic profiles in this radiograph (x-ray) of walnut (left to right): spoon bit, nose auger, Jennings bit. The threads of the lead screw are faintly visible on the bottom of the hole on the right. Compressed wood shows darker.

Holes made by a center bit are similar to those made by a Jennings bit, but like the nose auger, they leave only a single blade "stop."

[opposite]
Three spiral augers (left to right): Jennings bit with down-cutting lips (left), Gedge pattern bit with up-curving lips (center), and rare triple-bladed Scotch auger with right-angled, up-turned lips (right).

century. Larger sizes will not start on a surface unless a shallow pocket cut is first made for it with a gouge. In very tough wood, such as elm, it produces a distinct unbroken shaving like a rotini pasta. These shavings may sometimes be discovered in builders' debris. The bottom of a nose auger hole is slightly concave and shows a single radial "stop" of the single blade where cutting ceased. There should be no small central hole or cutter marks on the perimeter.

Center bit. Center bits appear in the French encyclopedias of the eighteenth century, but I cannot establish when they were first used in this country. They were common, however, after 1800. Because they lack any means to clear the chips from the hole, they are restricted to shallow work. Although there are two-bladed variants, center bits are generally distinguished by the presence of a single radial "stop," as well as by the central hole left by the pike and the scored perimeter left by the spur opposite the blade.

Spiral auger. The spiral auger with lead screw is commonly attributed to Phineas Cooke, who was awarded a prize of thirty guineas on May 1, 1770, for his invention. Many American patents for tools employing this innovation were issued around 1800 when new manufacturing techniques were developed. Still, the new augers are rare before 1810. The spiral auger commonly has two cutting blades which show as two radial stops divided by the hole left by the lead screw. Perimeter scoring lips or spurs appeared before the American Civil War, but augers with these additions were more expensive and less common. A mid-nineteenth-century variant called the Gedge pattern produces rounded, dished hole bottoms. Another type of spiral auger used by shipwrights lacks lead screw and spur and has but a single cutter. Its marks are similar to, but slightly more angular than, those left by the nose auger.

Dog bites and clamp marks. The end grain of small-dimensioned stock occasionally shows the marks of the bench dog or stop used to restrain the wood during planing. These marks can serve to link several different

The bite of the bench dog.

pieces of work to a specific workbench. Marks left by iron screw clamps are misleading, as they are often the work of careless modern restorers rather than the original craftsman.

Planes. Plane work is distinguished by its regularity. As in axes, nicks in the plane iron leave distinctive traces, a phenomenon known as "writing its name." This fingerprint lasts only until the next sharpening, but can be useful in linking a single tool to separate products. When the plane iron is not well supported by the body of the plane, it may repeatedly flex and spring back across the wood. This "chatter" leaves its distinctive marks only on the work cut by the face of the iron, and not on the surfaces created by the passage of its edge. Thus, the orientation of the plane can be determined and its type deduced.

Waffle face. The waffle face hammer is often thought to be a modern innovation. It is, however, a common early feature of hatchets used in preparing the lathing of a room prior to plastering. Such tools have been found in excavations that date to the seventeenth century.

Compass marks. When they can be positively identified, the points and arcs left by a compass (dividers) can indicate the nature of the design process. Dimensions for a given object may be derived from a template or from a formula of proportions which is determined and marked by steps of the compass. Templates or gauges bearing small iron points are also used in layout work, particularly in chairmaking. The marks made by these points can be mistaken for those left by the compass.

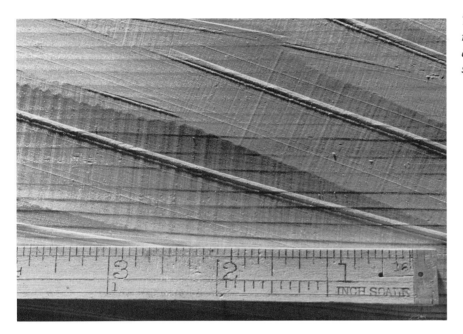

The plane iron that made these marks was ground convex and nicked; the chattering was the result of a poorly supported cutting edge.

[above]
When not pacing off measurements, the compass may be employed in gauging, as on the bottom of this window.

[left]
The waffle-faced hammer marks on this timber could have been made by a lath hatchet such as that shown in Moxon's 1678 Mechanick Exercises.

Numbers and letters cut by a timber scribe are often found on cooperage. Like a brand burned into the wood, these marks are difficult to remove.

Timber scribe. These tools are common from the eighteenth century on. They combine pull gouges with pikes to enable the user to cut letters and numbers into a surface. The pike allows one of the gouge arms to act like the arm of a compass for marking the circular portions of letters and numbers.

Pit saw. Pit sawing can be recognized by changes in the angle of the stroke at regular intervals of approximately one foot. The marks may be extremely regular and perpendicular to the length of the board, but will of necessity change as the top sawyer steps backward to avoid cutting himself in half. Although extremely rare, primitive hand-fed water-powered saws may produce similar variations. Pit sawing lingered longer in many areas and can be used for dating materials only after careful local research.

Experienced sawyers leave regular, almost vertical marks. The angle must shift every foot or so as the top man steps back.

[opposite]
A sash mill, as illustrated in 1650.

MACHINERY

Unlike hand tools, woodworking machinery represents a major investment that must be offset by economies of scale. A single machine can produce material that is distributed over a wide area. Legal documents or advertisements confirming the establishment of a mill in an area are more reliable than patent dates. Some quite sophisticated machinery (planers, tenoners, and so forth) was developed by the British Admiralty prior to 1800. Yet problems of cost and technology prevented their widespread use in this country until after the Civil War.

The marks from a sash mill vary more often in their spacing than in their angles.

Band-sawn surfaces exhibit widely spaced repeating patterns. These are generally post–Civil War.

Late-nineteenth-century American double circular saw.

Sash mill. Water-powered reciprocating saws mounted in vertically sliding frames were built in the New World in the first years of colonization. In places where the population was widely dispersed from water mill sites, the costs of transportation could outweigh the economic efficiency of the mill, and sawing would continue to be done by hand. Later sash mills were powered by horse or steam power, which allowed them to move to where the timber was rather than stay where the water power was. Depending on the feed mechanism used, the regular marks of the saw teeth may become much closer together when passing through a knot in the wood, indicating slower progress. Unlike pit saw marks, sash mill marks are parallel down the entire length of the log.

Band mill. Although the idea was patented in 1808, problems in welding the endless loop of the blades held back practical band saws until the 1840s. The marks left by band milling are difficult to distinguish from sash sawing. Although a continuous feed into the unbroken band of teeth should produce an even texture on the wood, inevitably some kink in the system leaves regularly spaced irregularities. Because the band saw blade must be about three times longer than a sash saw blade, the spacing on these irregularities is about three times wider.

Circular saw. The arc of circular saw marks is one of the commonest indicators of post-eighteenth-century work. Although the circular saw was developed for the British Admiralty in the 1770s, the largest diameter blade listed in Joseph Smith's 1816 *Key* is only 36 inches, which means that the saw was unable to handle timber more than about 16 inches thick. This problem was overcome by using circular blades in tandem, one below and one above.

Planer. The original mechanical planers from 1791 that imitated the reciprocating stroke of hand planing apparently saw little use. Transverse planing machines developed in 1802 used cutters mounted on arms on the end of a rapidly spinning shaft. As the timber advanced beneath them, the spinning cutters swept across the grain, leaving smooth transverse arcs similar to those left by the circular saw. These machines, commonly known as Daniels planers, were used more in heavy manufacturing than in preparing building or furniture stock. The rotary cylinder planer was well developed by 1828 when William Woodworth's patent began his "odious monopoly" of the machine. As there is no earlier device that could leave such marks, the distinctive cross-grain ripple left by slamming planer knives is a prime indicator of post-1800 work.

Circular saw marks may date from the early nineteenth century, but became common after the Civil War.

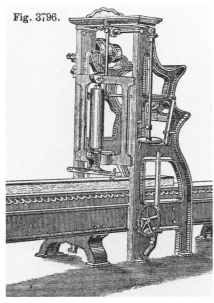

Fig. 3796.

[above]
*Daniel's transverse planer, illustrated in
Knight's 1876* American Mechanical
Dictionary.

[right]
*Severe rippling caused by a maladjusted
rotary planer. These marks are usually
much more subtle.*

10 THE FORT

*Construct a fort adjacent to ye town sufficient
to protect yr people. . . .*

—Ivor Noël Hume, memo to the author, 1983

THINGS were mirror backwards that May morning, the same but turned around. I stood on the cold muddy bluffs looking out over the James River reading my page of instructions ingeniously compiled from seventeenth-century documents by archaeologist Ivor Noël Hume. With these references confirmed by the archaeological evidence, the crew and I were to reconstruct the fort at the newly unearthed English settlement at Martin's Hundred. We were to work as the colonists might have worked, using the tools they might have used and thinking as they might have thought. My home was behind me, though, miles inland. To the strangers here in 1620, home was far down the river and further across the sea. It is a haunted place to me, but to them it was a bridgehead of security on the edge of wildness.

Let all your posts "be 10 inches square, and not to stand above 9 foot asunder, to be done with three rails between every post, of fitt scantling."

The story of the discovery of the fort is excitingly told in Noël Hume's book *Martin's Hundred*. Earlier searchers for seventeenth-century forts sought evidence of pointed-log forts in the "Fort Apache" mold. The evidence here, however, plainly indicated that this fort was a post and rail structure, presumably covered "with a strong pale of seven foot and a half height." Such a fence once protected the English colony of Dublin in Ireland; the wild Irish were kept outside, "beyond the pale."

Had these been Swedish or German colonists, they might have built log cabin–style blockhouses. Being English, however, and coming from a timber-starved island, they spoke only the language of frame construction. These Englishmen who waded ashore carried toolboxes not only on their shoulders but in their minds as well. They were equipped with the mental tools to solve problems in the same way they had solved them in another land, where the rules were quite different. But conservative as they might be, adaptation to this environment was a matter of necessity, not choice.

Make the holes for the said posts of sufficient depth and setting "the said posts at 9 foot distance one from the other and three foot in the ground, ramming stones and earth in the holes."

The only remaining evidence of the fort was that which had penetrated the earth beyond the reach of the plow. Two centuries of wheat, corn, and soybean cropping had erased all but the bottoms of the postholes. We began to dig these holes for the third time, following the colonist and the archaeologist. In the woods, now far away from the site, we felled white oaks, familiar timber to Englishmen, for the posts, rails, and pales of our fort. We put the broad-bladed American axes away and worked with the longer, narrower English tools. The size of the American trees had not yet wrought its changes on the ancient patterns.

[opposite]
The massacre of 1622, as imagined by German engraver Theodorus De Bry.

White oak timbers for the frame.

At any "Angle or Corner, where the lines meet, a Bulwarke or Watch-tower" shall be raised.

Although we did not fear attack by Indians or rival Spaniards from the south, for our own protection we had to build the watchtower first. The summer was hard. After a few hours of the Virginia heat you became either acclimated or dead. There was no shade for three hundred yards except what we could build for ourselves. In what little shade there was, the temperature was daily over 106 degrees, with humidity to match. On the worst days, only ten minutes' work exposure to the sun brought on a stupid madness. I recall being repeatedly asked if I was all right while singing forty minutes of "Funky Granny" punctuated by commercials for "Forts R Us."

All we knew of the watchtower was the spacing of the four posts of its corners: a 9-foot square, with perhaps a secure storeroom beneath the high platform where sentries could stand watch over both river and forest. We spaced the rails so that the middle set would support the joists for the platform of the watchtower.

The corner posts of the watchtower were a full 16 feet tall. Before we raised each post in its hole, we cut six mortices into it to hold the rails. We literally chopped the mortices into the green oak with twibils. One blade chopped across the grain on both ends of the mortice, while the other blade, in line with the grain, split out the wood in between. More than once the double-bitted, razor-sharp tools drew blood.

Truing the frame with plumb bob and Spanish windlass.

"Enclose y$_e$ whole work with bords. . . . They are to be cut sharp at y$_e$ tope & either listed or shot with a plaine." "The said pales are to be set and laid very close to one another, and pin the said pales and rails sloping downward with good and sufficient pins made of dry timber and strongly fastened in setting."

This business about getting the palings close together was no joke. One hopes that our ancestors with their matchlock muskets were somewhat humbled when they saw the Indians shoot flying birds out of the air with bows and arrows. I was fanatical about "listing" (trimming with a hatchet) the rough pales so that the contours fit perfectly against one another. Several of the fellows questioned the necessity of narrowing the gap to a quarter-inch maximum. But the planks were pegged up green; tight construction now would minimize problems later as the palings

The oak paling could be split in the forest and then carried back to the building site.

seasoned in the sun and shrank apart. It would take a lucky shot to nail you behind those walls.

Make the "Pallizado of Planckes and strong Posts . . . of yong Oakes, Walnuts, &c."

Trying to replicate today a structure that was originally built with oak from the virgin forest is about as easy as whipping up a passenger pigeon pie for supper. It wouldn't be much trouble if only you could find the stuff to work with. When an oak has grown for a few centuries in an ancient forest, its wood is mellow and straight grained. With axes, wedges, and mauls, a man could "fell, cut, lop, cleave and make up" a single huge tree into enough split planking to surround the entire perimeter of this fort. But these trees are gone. For them to return, everybody with European habits would have to leave the continent for about six hundred years to give the forest time to recover.

Although we all surmised that the fort was built with plank split from the virgin timber, there was no way we could attempt this at the time. We were already working on another series of large buildings that had to be covered in split oak. If we began competing with ourselves for this timber, neither job would be finished in time. Then again, our job is to attempt to explain historic behavior by experimental re-creations. Rebuilding the fort was intended as a landbound *Kon-Tiki*, not as an attempt to manifest a final conclusion.

So what was their alternative? What tools would they have had to work with? A 1622 English broadside addressing the problem of "the inconveniences that have happened to some persons which have transported Themselves from England to Virginia without provisions necessary to sustaine themselves" listed the following woodworking tools as essential for a family of six:

> Two broad Axes 3.s.8.d. a piece
> Five felling Axes 18.d. a piece
> Two steele hand sawes 16.d. a piece
> Two two-hand sawes 5.s. a piece
> One whip-saw, set and filed
>   with box, file, and wrest 10.s.
> Two hammers 12.d. a piece
> Two augers 6.d. a piece
> Sixe chissels 6.d. a piece
> Two percers stocked 4.d. a piece
> Three gimlets 2.d. a piece
> Two hatchets 21.d. a piece
> Two froues to cleave pale 18.d. a piece
> Two hand-bills 20.d. a piece
> One grindlestone 4.s.
> Nailes of all sorts to the value of 2£

*Russell Steele bores one of the hundreds
of peg holes needed to fasten the paling to
the rails. Bill Weldon works on the
doorway to the storeroom.*

If the residents of Martin's Hundred were so equipped, then they
would have been able to employ their ten-shilling "whip-saw" to saw,
rather than split, the palings. Could they—would they—have sawn
rather than split the pale? Our job was to find out. We sawed two
thousand square feet of white oak planking. Based on our experience, we
determined that it would have taken approximately one man-year (or
thirty men twelve days) to build the whole fort with pit-sawn timber. But
after actually doing it—after actually sawing that much paling in that

The watchtower takes shape.

stewpot over the James—I believe that they *could* have sawn out the pales, and—if they were really stupid—they *would* have.

> *"At each a Gate likewise to goe forth." And also make "gates of sawing timber of the best form and most substantialest manner, well hanged smooth and clear from rubbs of jutts of the ground."*

The gate is the weakest point of a wall. There the chain of rails is broken and the free end of the wall prone to waver. The load of the heavy

Nailing the poles on the rafters.

door also works against its post; each opening and closing works it looser in its hole. To counter this weakness, we ran heavy planks across the top, which also provided a modest protection for persons standing in the gateway.

The roof on the tower came last. Although we laid the spars for thatch, we made the first adaptation to the new land and covered the pyramid with cypress and tulip bark. Slicing green logs down one side, we peeled back the bark until it popped free. It was a favorite amusement of mine to step inside the cool cylinder of bark and imitate an ambulatory tree. We

The roof of sheets of cypress bark.

flattened the curled bark under timbers behind our saw pit in town. When it was dry, we simply nailed it onto the roof. No one is more surprised than I that this bark roof has survived two hurricanes without damage.

I now stand beneath this roof and I see an ironic American sampler from this wooden tower. Down the wide river, a distant forest of what appear to be dead pines is actually the congregated masts of an orphan fleet from the last big war—a hundred Liberty Ships chained bow to stern in a mile-square grid of floating corrosion. Straight across through the haze of river and pine forest, I can barely see the tops of twin domes where aggravated elements make our power. The huge orange warning sign where the waste heat is dumped into the river is but a dot on the distant tree-green bank. They joke of gigantic glow-in-the-dark crabs along this section of the river. On the flats between this timber fort and the shore, poison-preserved oak stubs outline the rectangular scars left on the land by the first injections of proto-Americans.

The native people were at first friendly with the newcomers. The English built this fort to defend against Spaniards attacking from the sea,

not against the Indians who shared their breakfast with them. But by that March morning in 1622, the native Americans had seen enough. They arose from the colonist's tables and proceeded to murder the new American families. They dragged off the survivors, leaving their English-style houses to burn to the ground.

Away from the river, up on the hill, however, it is not a village of reed-mat long houses that I see but a Georgian mansion, a great brick pile built of tobacco money. Back at the river's edge, New World ospreys and bald eagles dive for fish and rest in the skeleton of a great elm. The animals, and the river itself, are recovering from an industrial chemical poisoning inflicted years ago. Over my head, whiskered martins scratch about on the pyramidal roof. The distant whistle of an antique steam engine rolls slowly across the fields. The sound comes from a huge new theme park a mile up the river called "The Old Country." The puffing brass engine pulls a trainload of delighted Americans around a favorite section of the amusement park, a concrete fantasyland called "England."

11

THE BARN

. . . a house without Chimneys or partition and not one tittle of workmanship about it more than a Tobacco house.

—William Fitzhugh, 1686

LIKE a single remaining piece from a long-lost jigsaw puzzle, our tobacco barn is part of a nearly vanished system. We would soon be producing tobacco the old way at the restored eighteenth-century plantation of Carter's Grove, and without a proper barn the crop would be lost. We would build it in its traditional form for air curing the tobacco, a form which precisely followed its forgotten function. After the tobacco was picked, the harvesters skewered the individual leaves on sticks and hung them to dry for a while in the open air. The workers then loaded the sticks of leaves into the barn to cure. The sticks spanned the interior network of poles, the pendulous leaves not touching each other, yet filling the barn to the peak of the rafters,

The tobacco barn is like a filing cabinet. Rather than file folders, though, it suspends 4- or 5-foot-long split oak tobacco sticks. And just as filing cabinets must be constructed in different sizes to match legal or letter folders, tobacco barns are framed to match the sticks, in multiples of either 4 or 5 feet. Otherwise, these barns were very similar in construction and appearance. As William Tatham wrote in his *Essay on Tobacco* (1800), "One description may serve for every kind: they are so contrived as to admit poles in the nature of a scaffold through every part of them, ranging four feet from centre to centre, which is the length of the tobacco stick."

Scholars have studied wills, contracts, and other old records that gave dimensions for tobacco houses. They have discovered that barns based on 5-foot sticks (the length of the barn was evenly divisible by five, but not four) were more common in the early eighteenth century than they were later. One possible explanation for this is that the tobacco sticks were also hung between collar ties nailed to every other rafter pair. Thus, rafter spacing also had to follow the length of the tobacco stick. Five-foot sticks meant rafters on 2½-foot centers. Clapboards split from oak billets were the cheapest coverings for these barns, and because they were nailed directly to the rafters, clapboards of that length had to be made 5 feet long as well. This is just about the limit of convenient splitting, and as the higher quality virgin timber was used up, they got harder and harder to make. Four feet long (with 2-foot rafter centers) is an easier standard to live by. (I must mention here the Calvert County, Maryland, family who built their barns in 4 ½-foot bays so that no one could borrow their tobacco sticks.)

The barn we built belongs to yet another forgotten pattern. Beyond the essentials of sheltering and supporting the tobacco, the barn also had to fit the specific regional matrix of culture and environment. Although its roots are clearly set in English framing, this type of barn was raised in America, in a most un-English environment of abundant materials and scarce labor. The profligate use of massive white oak timbers, insane by English standards, was hardly seen as wasteful by men who wanted the forest cleared so that they could grow more tobacco. The lapped joints connecting the braces, posts, plates, and sills (there's not a proper mortice and tenon joint in the whole thing) were easier and faster for carpen-

Kerry Shackelford digs the post hole as Sarah Traband tends to the charring of the posts.

We used the twin-billed morticing axe to chop the open laps for the braces.

ters to cut. Sinking the posts in the ground added confidence to the uncertain bracing. The barn was constructed in the English language of carpentry, but with a strong twist of the Chesapeake vernacular.

The height of the barn was also figured by the leaf-laden stick. Tatham wrote that 12 feet was "indeed a good height for the larger crops; because this will allow four feet pitch each to three sucessive tiers of tobacco." Proper spacing was essential to admit "a free circulation of air . . . for the process of curing the plant." Because the foot-square posts would have to go at least 4 feet into the ground, we had to begin by cutting 16-foot logs to hew. A timber of fresh oak this size weighs about half a ton—and that is after it is hewn. Without the oxen, we would never have been able to move such timber. Even the oxen would have had a rough time without the two big wheels of the timber cart.

If there were no termites or fungi to recycle dead timber, the forests could live only a few decades before being buried by the weatherbeaten accumulation. Bugs and rot, however, are no keen respecters of property, and any dead timber within their reach is fair game. The sheer mass of the oak posts of the barn give a moderate assurance of longevity—there is simply more wood than the bugs can eat at one sitting. White oak heartwood is fairly rot resistant anyway, but we followed the common practice of charring the ends that were to go in the ground. Tests have long since proven that this does little good, but it apparently worked two hundred years ago—because all the two-hundred-year-old books say it did.

Beyond studying surviving barns of this type to determine their form, we also needed to know the process used to erect them. Archaeological evidence left by hole-set buildings gives us important clues. If all the holes left in the ground are oblong—that is, sloped away in the same direction—then one can surmise that the wall was framed on the ground and raised as a unit. The best indicator of which side it was raised from is the direction of the pegs. Pegs driven in after the frame is standing may come in from either direction. But pegs in a frame laid out on the ground must be driven in (obviously) from the top side down. Studies of the few hole-set barns that survived, and of the traces left by the postholes of those that did not survive, told us how walls were raised as units after having been assembled on the ground.

IMPORTANT PEOPLE

Working with the past does not make you immune to the realities of the present, and barns, hole set or otherwise, do not get built for free. Our work relies on foundations, and I don't mean the kind made from brick or stone. We must compete for funding just like a symphony or an art museum. Without our grants, we could do nothing, and the guardians of our benefactors' money are *important people* to us.

Normally, these people would not figure in this story, but my compulsion to please them had an early influence on the construction of this building. One morning, after two weeks of felling, hauling, hewing, and notching the massive timbers, we learned that some of them were going to stop by the next day to see how their money was being spent. Our informant strongly suggested that we had better have more to show than a huge pile of chips and ten big timbers on the ground.

We had already dug the holes at the site, but the rest of the framing timber was still standing in the woods with leaves on it. Overreacting as usual, I elected to go ahead and stand the posts in their holes individually and worry about the rest of the frame later. It was not the right way to raise the building, but it would give our benefactors something impressive to see.

All the rest of that day we canted the huge heavy posts into their holes in a series of Iwo Jima–style raisings. The notches in the posts had to line up perfectly to take the rest of the framing. When the two end posts were set plumb and true, we ran tight strings between them to guide the placement of the three middle ones. We levered them about, sometimes kicking more dirt in beneath them, sometimes lifting and dropping them in hopes of pounding them deeper. By the next morning, our version of Woodhenge was suitably impressive. Silly, but impressive.

Our "important people" came and went, leaving us with our posts in the air, our beams on the ground, and our funding intact. Now it was a

Raising one post at a time.

simple matter (ha!) of hoisting the 32-foot-long, 8 by 8 beams into place. One we just plain lifted into place in a daring move of brute strength and foolhardiness. The coopers who were nearby making hogsheads for the tobacco lent a welcome hand. For the other beam, we took the time to rig a gin pole and block and tackle. More actual work was involved, consid-

An upended joist and block and tackle for hoisting the second plate.

ering the preparation, but the hedge against potential excitement (getting crushed by a falling timber) was well worth it.

When the joists and rafters were in place our "important people" came to visit again. I invited them to climb up with me on the building to look around. Most folks get a big thrill from climbing up on an unfinished

Mark and Bill level the top of the plate to prepare it for the joists.

building. When they reached the top of the plate, I spotted a three-pound sledge hammer left on a joist. It was against our rules to leave a hammer where it might be knocked over. Although at the raising of the Vatican obelisk in 1586 "the carpenters wore iron helmets on their heads, to protect them," we work without hard hats for authenticity's sake—so rules about such hazards must be strict.

"This shouldn't be up here," I said, and pushed the sledge hammer off

the edge of the timber. At that exact instant, I saw Bill walk precisely beneath it. Fate could not have cut a closer hand between life and death. Bill was walking just fast enough that the hammer missed the back of his head by half an inch and fell into damp earth with a revolting SPLOK.

I still have nightmares.

Russ pegs the tilted false plate to the ends of the joists.

DISRAISING

Soon, the joists and tilted false plates were in place and the rafters raised over them. The 4 by 8 split oak bracing was inset deep into the sills. The posts were sunk 4 feet into the hard earth. Our barn promised sure defiance of any force that might try to move its frame. We reveled in the usual pride of accomplishment as we topped out our work with a toast of cheap champagne. Nothing could possibly disturb such a massively secure structure. Nothing, except . . . somebody important decided that the barn was in the wrong place.

We had better things to do than tear down and uproot a barn which we had just finished building. I stalled and argued, but there was no way around it. There had been a change in plans and the barn had to be moved to the far side of the apple orchard, about three hundred yards north. Other obligations kept us away, and the barn sat as a bare skeleton over the winter.

Late the following spring we returned to begin ripping the shingle lath off of the rafters of the barn. The exposure to the rain had so deteriorated the sweet gum false plates that they would have to be replaced. We lowered the timbers to the ground and stacked them to the side. Although the posts were set over 4 feet deep in the ground, they were the easiest to remove. The notches that held the sills just above ground level gave us lodgements for levers. We set short timbers a foot away from the posts for fulcrums, placed the 10-foot-long levers in the notches, and climbed aboard. The four of us bouncing in rhythm lifted the posts about 10 inches before the height of the fulcrum had to be increased. When there was no more than a foot of post remaining in the ground, one of us would give the post a push to send it toppling over to one side.

RESURRECTION

We soon finished moving the timbers and were ready to re-raise the barn in its new location. Because all of the timbers were ready, we could now raise complete walls rather than individual posts. We would assemble one wall, raise it, and then move in and assemble the timbers of the second wall. This time, however, the raising was not going to be a simple matter of push and grunt. Walls this heavy could only be raised with considerable rigging.

Parallel to the new location of the barn was a hedgerow of trees and a convenient red cedar that would provide a suitably high anchorage for a block and tackle. The tree was covered with a leafless, sinister web of poison ivy. I leaned a ladder up against a large limb and reached gingerly in to loop a double turn of line around the high fork in the trunk. While I was struggling with the ladder, though, Dan had bravely climbed straight up the side through the snapping twiggery. "I don't think you can get poison ivy when the leaves aren't out," he said as he took the rope from my hand and knotted it tight among the cracking vines. They released him from the hospital just in time for the raising.

The double-luff block and tackle had four pulleys on it and consequently multiplied our strength by five. The south wall of the barn was framed and sitting at about a ten-degree angle, ready to be tipped into its holes. Just to be sure that we would be able to raise the wall when the time came, the whole crew gathered and began to heave on the line. Nothing happened. The wall was so heavy that we could not move it. This could prove embarrassing. There was a museum conference in town, and two hundred of our colleagues from around the nation were going to be visiting the next day to help with the raising and join in the subsequent festivities. I was reluctant to use the oxen for the raising.

The day before we got the news.

They were new, and I was new to them. I felt sure about using them to drag logs out of the woods, but raising a building was another matter. The consequences of not stopping pulling at the right moment could be "intense."

We had already spent several hours anchoring the crab, the eight-man capstan that we used for heavy pulling, on the far side of the meadow to raise the north wall. It would take too long on raising day if we had to relocate it for each wall. Although we did not have enough cable to

"Of the Drug, and Its Use"

The Drug described in Plate 9.A. is made somewhat like a low narrow Carr. It is used for the carriage of Timber, and then is drawn by the Handle, by two or more Men, according as the weight of the Timber may require.
—Joseph Moxon 1678
Mechanick Exercises

We were fortunate to have a wheelwright who could build a timber cart for us. Without it we would still be in the woods. We use it as much to carry timber on top of it as we do to haul logs slung underneath it. It even helps us to lift the timber by acting as a wheel-mounted lever. We run a chain around the tail end of the shaft and the log on the ground, tilt the handle end up, tighten the chain, and then pull the handle end down. When the log is lifted as close to the shaft as possible, we chain the front end. If we have the log properly balanced, off we go.

Moxon's "drug."

Our timber cart, a "carrylog" based on Moxon's.

A more advanced version is found in Denis Diderot's 1763 *Encyclopédie*. It uses a lever-action chain hoist and is intended to be drawn by a horse. Diderot also showed a hand-drawn timber cart called the *diable* in his illustration of carpenters at work.

We use a different sort of "yard truck" on our jobs, one that is based on those described by Henry Mercer in his 1929 *Ancient Carpenter's Tools*. Also called a "drug," it consists of a locust roller, an iron axle, and a frame of three pieces of heavy elm. Because of the difficulties of boring a perfectly centered hole through a large cylinder, we chopped the locust roller true to the axle only after the two were assembled. I joined the frame with paired mortice and tenon joints, flaring the mortices slightly on the outside so that the joints could be locked into place by wedges driven in from outside.

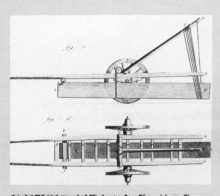

[left]
Diderot's timber cart.

[right]
The yard truck.

[left]
The "Diable."

[right]
Boring out the axle hole for a new locust roller.

Frank chars the timbers of the north wall on the day of the second raising. The south wall in the background is ready to raise with lines reaching to pullies in the cedar tree.

[opposite]
The crab anchored to a "dead man," a timber buried in a trench. Similar archaeological features were discovered near this site.

stretch to it from the cedar tree, one of the fellows convinced me that he could make long running splices and build up a long line that would be strong enough to hold.

The next day the spliced line ran from the crab to the block and tackle in the cedar tree. Tied to the moving end of the block and tackle were four lines which ran to the top plate of the wall. This moving block and its tie lines were suspended by a bipod of heavy pine poles, which would cause the rope to lift the frame rather than pull it backwards during the first half of its journey from horizontal to vertical.

The time arrived. Our two hundred "museum people" gathered and were divided up into teams. Eight people worked the crab and, on command, began walking in their circle, stepping high over the rope where it led onto and off of the drum. Three men kept tension on the line, one pushed with a pole to correct the feed onto the drum, and others stood ready with snub lines to keep the wall from falling over once it was up. The frame creaked and ropes twanged like the strings of bass fiddles as the first wall frame slowly rose. Everything worked as planned.

The feet of the posts slid against heavy planks set on the far walls of the holes to keep them from digging in. When the frame was past forty-

The Crab

I had been away for a few days but it was no surprise to me when I saw that Russ had made a "crab" or capstan while I was gone. They usually get a lot more done when I am away. He had taken some old oak timbers to make the frame and a huge locust log to make the roller. We were going to need the crab to raise the frame of the tobacco barn. Just how badly we would need it I had no idea.

At the time there was a monstrous pine log that the oxen had brought in. We were going to hew it and then pit saw it into the sills for a job in town.

The timber was so heavy that there was no way we would be able to lift it onto the trestles at the job site; so I figured that after it was hewn we would hitch up the team and haul the log over to the sawpit. But I had not figured on what would happen the next time I went away. While I was gone, Russ had rigged up a tripod with pulleys and cable and they had hoisted the monster up on the straining trestles. I never thought it possible.

I wondered at the name "crab." The lever arms radiate spokelike from it like the legs of a crab, but the best explanation became apparent when we had to move the heavy thing. Tying a long cable to a tree in the general direction we wanted to go in, we walked around in a circle, winding up the cable and pulling the crab along. Because it was not anchored by its tail, the frame began to turn until the upright on the side stopped the movement. It continued to pull along sideways, just in the manner of a crab.

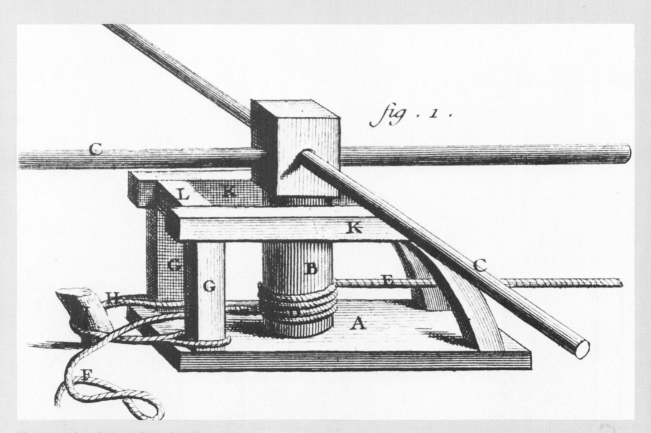

The capstan from Diderot's Encyclopédie.

The south wall with but a few degrees to go.

five degrees, the lines from the cedar tree ran straight and the bipod fell away. Thirty people with shovels were standing by, waiting for the signal. When the wall at last was upright and plumb, I called out, "Dirt crew, have at it!" I barely had time to pull the planks out from behind the posts before they rushed in to send dirt flying into the holes, freezing the posts in the ground.

When the south wall was secure, the team in charge of the second frame moved their timbers into position. We had placed the posts and beams on rollers the day before, and they were relatively easy to move. I had not foreseen the excitement that would be a natural part of such an event, and traffic jams developed between competing timber drivers. Finally the frame was puzzled together and levered into position. A bucket of oak pegs appeared and for about five minutes the fields echoed with sound of twenty lusty, dusty men and women pounding with whatever makeshift hammers they could find.

Meanwhile, the crab crew removed the block and tackle from the cedar tree, carried it to the other side of the barn, and anchored it to the base of the crab itself. They retied the lines to the newly assembled north wall and reset the bipod. Everyone was feeling his oats, and the last knot was no sooner tied than the crab crew began their quickstep march. I watched from the side so that I could call for them to stop at the moment that the frame was vertical. The wall began to rise without a hitch, the bipod fell away as it should, and the crab crew began to sing "Drunken Sailor" in vigorous cadence.

The spectacle was transfixing as the huge timber frame closed the final few degrees to plumb. Everyone else must have been under the spell of the moving mass, because when I shouted, "Ready on the snub lines!" they seemed to wake with a start and gave the line a heavy jerk.

The north wall, ninety seconds before the rope broke.

The weathered gray hemp of the snub line would probably have broken in any case, but the jerk caused the bowline knot to snap at the worst possible moment.

I know I shouted something as I watched the seven-ton oak frame suddenly accelerate past the vertical, mousetrapping straight for a cluster of well-dressed people who had broken unnoticed from the crowd to take some dramatic photographs of the raising. I glimpsed the crab crew out of the corner of my eye, frantically turning the crab backwards, as though the slackening rope would somehow push back the wall.

Suddenly the wall stopped and the snub line pulled taut. The remains of the broken knot had snagged in one of the lap joints. "Don't anyone go near that wall. Don't anyone on those ropes make a move!" I shouted. Everyone was frozen and hardly needed me to tell them to stand still. The wall was hanging by a rotten thread. The rafters were piled on the far side of the barn and I began a circuitous trot toward them, bounding along as lightly as I could for fear that the vibration might send the wall smashing down.

"Get some rafters," I said as I ran. Several people with the same thought had shouldered rafters and were moving in to prop up the frame

before I even reached the pile. Someone pushed a new rope into my hands and I gingerly tossed it over the plate. The crab crew had the presence of mind to take up their abundant slack before we pulled the wall back upright. It was a considerably warier dirt crew that filled in around the posts on this wall.

The rest of the frame went up that afternoon without incident. That night there was music, a roast pig, dancing, and celebration. Everyone had a marvelous time, still bubbling with enthusiasm for the day's adventures.

I went home early.

12 THE FORGE

"I frame no hypotheses."
—Sir Isaac Newton, 1675

THE golfer hears a noise. Suddenly six dirt-covered, sweat-soaked men in knee breeches burst from the woods. Four carry axes on their shoulders; two lead a span of oxen, which in turn pull an overloaded two-wheeled timber cart. They crash down the hill and onto the road. He misses the two-foot putt.

These are good times. Riding the logs to keep them balanced as we climb the hill into town, we can talk and joke without worrying about being "out of character." From a distance it looks and sounds right. The language is a little different, but the laughter is the same.

One of us runs ahead to stop traffic on Francis Street as we enter the historic area of Colonial Williamsburg. We reach the timber yard and dump the fresh pine logs, heavy and sticky with sap on their ends. Soon the string lines snap down the length of the brown bark. The axeman stands atop the log to start his rhythmic chopping and splitting. The people gather, and the reconstruction of James Anderson's blacksmith shops begins.

THE PLAN

Anderson's blacksmith shops were originally built with no more thought than a turtle gives to its shell. They were built during the War for Independence to supply the Continental government and army with the iron work that had formerly been coming from England. Few structures, however, have had the benefit of such extensive research and planning as did its reconstruction. In 1982 all that remained of James Anderson's wartime workshop were a few bricks of its foundations. Only enough archaeological evidence survived to indicate the location of forges, the outlines of the 90-foot-long structure, and the chronology of its four stages of construction. We lacked even a good example of this sort of building. Understandably, no Revolutionary War–era wood-frame blacksmith shops have survived to our time.

Few buildings have also been the source of such controversy. Our reconstruction had to be based on bits and pieces of information, a window from here, rafter framing from there, that could be fitted together into a reasonable whole. It was unrealistic to expect that everyone should agree, and the arguments continued. Perhaps a sill was too high, a room too dimly lit by the small windows, or the door trim too fancy. But the building was an experiment; Sir Isaac Newton's "I-do-not-frame-hypotheses" attitude would have had to change if he wanted a job with us.

"Gentlemen, you have two minutes remaining!" called out the man with the gold watch.

"Sir," I answered as I drove home the last peg, "we (*bang!*) are (*bang!*) done (*bang!*)"

Russ and Frank precut the notches for the chimney headers in the gable end rafters.

The crowd went wild. We had completed framing the first section of Anderson's blacksmith shops in just under the two-hour limit of our wager. Perhaps I should not have promised them all a share of the reward—the bottle went round and was empty before I could reach it.

The building went up so fast because it was already built. Each wall, each floor, each rafter pair had previously been framed together with mortice and tenon joints, the peg holes bored, and then disassembled to wait until raising day. It's like a house of cards, fabricating one card at a time, and then putting them all together. The raising was simply a matter of reassembling the numbered timbers flat on the ground, gathering all the help that we could, connecting the walls, and putting it up.

Raising.

In the dangerous jobs close to the frame were craftsmen from all over town. Everyone was helping, though. The ropes tied to the wall frames were pulled by some of the hundreds of people who came to share in the event. Throughout the entire project, we enlisted help in pulling crosscut saws, driving wedges, chopping mortices, shaving clapboards, glazing windows, or whatever needed doing. For at least the next seventy-five years, the blacksmiths working in these shops will be interrupted by people pointing out boards that they planed or joints that they helped cut.

Sharing and teaching as you work is not for everyone, though. The site became a favorite of escorts conducting school groups through the historic area. The unrelenting pressures of visitation, construction dead-

Now the rafters.

lines, solving new problems, and mastering old skills can take their toll. Consider the joys of the apprentice working on his very first window (seventy-eight tenon shoulders and scribed joints that must meet perfectly before dark) and looking up to find himself facing his seventeenth group of fifth graders today that (in the words of their escort) "would just love to help you!"

LEARNING

Even before the first tree was felled, the project began to teach us about early construction practices. Before we could begin, I had to estimate how long it would take us to find, fell, and haul the trees to town—and then split, hew, saw, plane, and frame them into a 20-by-90-foot blacksmith shop. Just as spinning the thread and weaving the fabric for a shirt takes much longer than the tailoring, preparing our material from the forests to the south of town was going to take much longer than the actual carpentry.

But how to figure it? This was not your everyday building of store-bought stock. We had the trees; what would cost us was the labor to cut

them up. Eventually, I arrived at a computer spreadsheet program that accounted for every board and timber in the building, calculated the *surface* area of each piece in square feet, and then multiplied this by a time factor based on our experience in axe swinging, ox driving, and pit saw pulling.

Later, looking through some eighteenth-century housebuilding estimates, I noticed for the first time that estimates then were calculated in exactly the same manner. Today, of course, commercial builders pay for timber by its volume. But two centuries ago, when materials were relatively abundant and labor relatively dear, builders charged for timber by the *superficial foot*, the proper measure of the work that went into slicing it up, rather than by how much wood was there. With great labor, I had arrived at a system on my computer identical to that used with quill on paper two centuries earlier.

THE MATERIAL WORLD

As in any building job, the first material we cut was that which needed to be the driest. Framing can be relatively unseasoned, but floorboards and

The jug was empty.

joinery stock must be dry when they go into place. Thus, the last to be used must be the first that is cut.

We were used to pit sawing, priding ourselves as a hard-cutting crew, but never before had we produced so much stock that needed to seasoned under cover. We quickly found that we had no place to store our accumulating piles of five-quarter (⁵⁄₄ inch thick) pine boards. We managed to secure the use of the loft of a neighbor's barn, stacking the planks on hastily riven stickers to let the air circulate. Even so, there was not enough ventilation, and the fresh sapwood was quickly black with mildew and stain. The soot of the blacksmith's fires would cover that soon enough, though.

Because the original building was built in four stages during the war, we devised numerous details to indicate the different periods of construction. The sawn-through braces and empty mortices of removed walls would be easy to spot, but one of the more subtle distinguishing features was the method used to "gauge in" the flooring. To lay a level floor of hand-sawn boards of uneven thickness, they must be adzed to the thickness of the thinnest board wherever they cross joists. This leaves the top surface level and lets the "fat" hang down below. To guide the adzing, there are three common ways of gauging the boards. The first method uses a carpenter's gauge and a rabbet plane to establish the guidelines for the adze. We used the other two methods, one in each of the two shops with upper floors.

The first shop floor was gauged in the English manner, using a sash fillister plane to cut a small rabbet at a constant width from what would be the upper surface. For the second shop floor, we used a method we found in Southampton County, Virginia. We first scratched the constant line with a marking gauge and then drawknifed a bevel down to the line.

Finding the wood to make clapboards from was a major problem. Our reconstruction of Anderson's shops is covered, roof and sides, with thousands of 4-foot-long split oak boards. In the colonial period, these were the cheapest building materials you could make or buy. When farmers were constantly clearing new land for crops, they could send their boys to clear off the trees and split them into clapboards. Relatively unskilled people with simple tools—just wedges, a maul, and a froe—could produce enough clapboards from a single tree to cover a house. They could then sell the clapboards to builders for much less than sawn boards. But . . . that was when trees were *trees*.

My search for clapboard trees, equivalents of the virgin timber of the colonial forest, led me literally from the mountains to the sea. Occasionally, I would get calls from people that had heard that I was looking for really big trees. "By gum," they had "the biggest damn trees you ever saw!" Inevitably they turned out actually to be gum, or their idea of big was about 16 inches in diameter. Finally, I ended up in timber yards, actively bidding against buyers from Germany and Japan. A single 30-

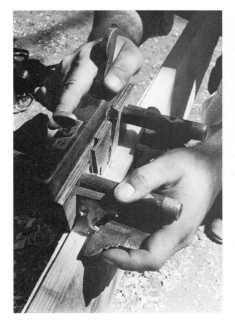  

inch log of prime white oak could cost over a thousand dollars, but it would cover half the roof—and it was sweet stuff to work. "Boys," I would say as I brought such a log into the yard, "I brought you some candy."

NAILS

Somehow I never was able to make a firm estimate of how many nails we needed. I could have done so easily by simply expanding on my estimates of the boards. Yet every few weeks we would hit the bottom of the keg and someone would have to walk down to the Deane forge on the other end of town to get more. I now think that the chance to escape the yard and walk through the streets on a legitimate mission was too valuable to sacrifice for mundane efficiency.

All the nails were made by the same blacksmiths who would be moving into Anderson's when it was completed. As each new smith took up nail making, you could see his skills improve. Even on something as small and simple as a nail you can read the confidence and proficiency of the hand that made it. From awkward, stubby spikes they quickly grew lean and wise like little El Greco monks.

I learned to use the nails better as well. All the old T-headed nails that we found had the ends flattened to a spade point in the same plane as the arms of the T. The T-headed nails were intended as finishing nails, the arms of the T to be sunk in with the grain of the wood. When it was

[left]
Each floorboard has to be gauged with the sash fillister plane, . . .

[middle]
. . . adzed out over each joist, . . .

[right]
. . . and then sprung into place for a tight fit.

Russ rives some of the thousands of oak clapboards.

[opposite]
Although the sides could be red oak, only the impervious white oak would do for the roof.

aligned with the grain, however, the spade point made the nails particularly prone to splitting the wood. I ended up boring a lot of holes with gimlets before I discovered the trick. If the spade point is started across the grain, the wood will not split and the nail will twist in the wood to align itself *with* the the grain by the time the head is driven flush. Little iron Zen masters going with the flow.

Once the boards were on, we painted each roof with pure pine tar cut half and half with turpentine. It's more like a black varnish than tar, but

[right]
Frank could work on the peak by standing on boards laid on the collar beams of the rafters.

[left below]
Russ evens the edges.

[right below]
The batten doors held by wrought spikes, clenched "dead as a doornail."

Only the resinous heart of yellow pine will last as an unpainted window.

Frank frames in a staircase header in the joists of the addition.

still very sticky. You can tell the exact season of the year when we tarred each section of the roof. We coated the first roof in early summer. I don't know if it was the smell or the gloss of the fresh tar that proved so attractive to flying *insecta*, but like an aerial La Brea tar pit, our roof cleansed the air of June bugs for miles around. Their shells still pebble the roof like sparse pavement. We finished the adjoining roof in October. Somehow every leaf from every tree in town heard about it and flew directly to us. Our roof was flocked in foliage.

Russ chisels a slot for a window sill in one of the peeled pine poles used for studs in the south wing.

After checking the post with the plumb rule, they will inset the brace from the outside. This method is faster and cheaper than the fully housed brace joints used in the first section of the shop.

You can touch the past sometimes. The field research took us to ancient corners, crawling with flashlight and ruler through dust-covered attic framing in distant counties. Each scratch and tool mark on the timbers recorded an unremembered instant of judgment and sweat. We spoke quietly as we interpreted their meanings. Ghosts were watching.

The past can come after you, too. I sat by the shop one twilight June evening as the moon rose. Abruptly, a great mud turtle the size of a soup tureen crawled from under a stack of clapboards. It could only have come

The north wing rafters—split from heart of oak.

from the stream to the south across Francis Street. The turtle had apparently spent the day under the boards waiting for the thousands to depart. As I watched, it went straight north across the yard until it was stopped by the bolted gate that led onto Duke of Gloucester Street.

I figured that the turtle was on some ancient ancestral mission to reach the stream behind the Printing Office and the York River drainage. To do so now, it would have to get through this gate, cross the street which was now open to cars, and descend fifteen very steep steps. I picked up the turtle, vaulted the fence, carried it across the street and down the steps, and set it in the water. I climbed back up the dark steps and walked back to the shop in the moonlight. I checked the lock on the tool shed and looked back at the shop. Turtles must have been crossing at this point for ten thousand years.

One morning I had the help of a half-dozen people crosscutting pine logs in the cool sunlight. A father was teasing his small sons with mock threats of no supper until they had all the wood cut. I was enjoying the scene when a man suddenly laughed and turned to me with watery eyes and a contorted smile.

"It's funny how people see different things," he said in heavy Eastern

European accents. "These people see fun for their children cutting this wood. I remember when I was a boy we were prisoners during the war and made to cut trees in the forest."

"Do you see that fungus?" He pointed to a sick-looking extrusion from a rotting log. "You would not see that, but we would have fought each other to get that fungus to have food to eat. Even now, I see that and before I could think, I was moving to take it before you could."

I looked at him. He knew that I did not know what to say. He reached out and shook my hand.

"You are doing good work here," he said. "This is a good thing."

We stood silently watching the laughing family for a few minutes before he nodded to me and walked on.

APPENDIX

Original Text of *The Debate of the Carpenter's Tools*

The shype ax seyd vnto þe wryght,
'Mete & drynke I schalle þe plyght,
Clene hose & clene schone,
Gete þem wer as euer thou kane;   4
Bot fore all þat euer þou kane,
Thall neuer be thryfty man,
Ne none þat longes þe crafte vnto,
Fore no thyng þat thou kane do.'   8
  'Wherefore,' seyd þe belte,
'With grete strokes I schalle hym pelte;
My mayster schall full welle thene
Both to cloþe & fede his men.'   12
  'Ʒe, ʒe,' seyd þe twybylle,
'Thou spekes euer ageyn skylle;
I-wys, i-wys, it wylle not bene,
Ne neuer, I thinke, þat he wylle thene.'   16
  'Ʒis, ʒis,' seyd þe wymbylle,
'I ame als rounde as a thymbyll;
My maysters werke I wylle remembyre;
Y schall crepe fast in-to þe tymbyre   20
And help my mayster within a stounde
To store his cofere with xx pounde.'
  'Ʒe, ʒe,' seyd þe compas,
'Thou arte a fole in þat case,   24
For þou spekes without vysment;
Therefore þou getyst not þi entent;
Wyte þou wele it schall be so
That lyghtly cum schall lyghtly go;   28
An þou gete more than oþer fyue,
ʒit schall þi mayster neuer thryue.'
  The groping iren than spake he,
'Compas, who hath grevyd þe?   32
My mayster ʒit may thryue full wele;
How he schall I wylle þe telle:
I ame his seruant, trew & gode,
Y suere þe, compas, by þe rode;   36
Wyrke I schalle boþe nyght & dey
To gete hym gode I schall assey.'
  'Ʒe, ʒe,' seys þe saw,
'Yt is bote bost þat þou doyst blow,   40
Fore thofe þou wyrke bothe dey & nyght
He wyll not the, I sey þe ryght;
He wones to nyʒe þe ale wyffe
And he thouht euer fore to thryffe.'   44
  Than seyd þe whetstone:
'Thoff my mayster thryft be gone,
Y schall hym helpe within þis ʒere
To gete hym xx^ti merke clere;   48

Hys axes schall I make fulle scharpe
That þei may lyʒhtly do þer werke;
To make my master a ryche mane
I schall asey, if þat I canne.'   52
  To hym þan seyd þe adys
And seyd, 'Ʒe, ser, God glades,
To speke of thryfft it wyll not be
Ne neuer, I thinke, þat he schall the;   56
Fore he wylle drynke more on a dey
Than þou cane lyghtly arne in twey;
Therefore þi thonge I rede þou hold
And speke no more no wordes so bold.'   60
  To þe adys than seyd þe fyle,
'Thou schuldes not þi mayster reuyle,
Fore thoff he be vnhappy,
ʒit fore his thryft þou schuldes se;   64
Fore I thinke or tomorow at none
To arne my mayster a pyre of schone;
Fore I schalle rube with all my myght
My mayster tolys forto dyght,   68
So þat with-in a lytell space
My mayster purce I schall encrece.'
  Than seyd þe chesyll,
'And euer he thryue, he berys hym wele;   72
Fore tho þou rube to þi hede ake,
His thryfte fro hym it wyll be take;
Fore he loues gode ale so wele
That he þerfore his hod wyll selle;   76
Fore some dey he wyll vij^d drynke;
How he schall thryue I canne not thinke.'
  'Ʒe, ʒe,' seyd þe lyne & þe chalke,
'My mayster is lyke to many folke;   80
Tho he lufe ale neuer so wele,
To thryu & the I schall hym telle;
Y schall merke well vpone þe wode
And kepe his mesures trew & gode;   84
And so by my mesures all
To the full wele my mayster schall.'
  Than bespake þe pryking knyfe,
'He duellys to nyʒe þe ale wyfe;   88
Sche makes oft-tyme his purse full thynn;
No peny some tyme sche leuye þerin;
Tho þou gete more than oþer thre,
Thryfty man he canne not be.'   92
  'Ʒe, ʒe,' seyd þe persore,
'That þat I sey it schall be sure;
Whi chyd ʒe iche one with oþer?
Wote ʒe not wele I ame ʒour broþer?   96

Therefore none contrary me,
Fore as I sey so schall it be;
My mayster ʒit schall be full ryche,
Als fere as I may stret & streche;   100
Y wyll helpe with all my myght
Both by dey & by nyght,
Fast to runne in to þe wode
And byte I schall with moth full gode;   104
And þus I trow be my crowne
To make hym schyreff of þe tounne.'
    'Sof, ser,' seyd þe skantyllʒon,
'Y trow ʒour thryft be wele ny done;   108
Euer to crewyll þou arte in word;
And ʒet þou arte not worth a tord!
Fore all þe gode þat þou gete myght,
He wyll spend it on a nyght.'   112
    Than þe crow bygane to speke
Fore-why is herte was lyke to breke,
To here his broþer so reuyld
And seyd, 'þou spekes lyke a chyld!   116
Tho my mayster spend neuer so faste,
Y-nouʒe he schall haue at þe laste
May forteyne as mych as euer shall he
That drynke neuer peny to þat he dyʒe.'   120
    'ʒe, ʒe,' seyd þe rewle,
'Y-feyth þou arte bot a fole!
Fore & he dyʒe & haue ryght nouʒht,
Who trowys þou wyll gyfe hym owght?   124
Thus schall he ly vpone þe grownd
And be beryd lyke an hund;
Fore & a man haue ought before,
When he has nede it is gode store.'   128
    'What, ser reule,' seyd þe pleyn,
'Anoþer reson I wyll þe seyne;
Thoff my mayster haue no happe,
ʒit þi mayster þou schudyst not lake;   132
Fore ʒit a mene I schall se
That my mayster schall wele the;
Y schall hym helpe both dey & nyght
To gete hym gode with all my myght;   136
Y schalle clens on euery syde
To helpe my mayster in his pride.'
    The brode ax seyd, withouten mysse,
He seyde, 'þe pleyn my broþer is;   140
We two schall clence & make full pleyne,
That no man schall vs geyne-seyne;
And gete oure mayster in a ʒere
More syluer than a man may bere.'   144
    'ʒe, ʒe,' seyd þe twyuete,
'Thryft I trow be fro ʒou fette
To kepe my mayster in his pride;
Yn þe contre ʒe canne not byde   148
Without ʒe stele & be thefys
And put meny men to greffys;
Fore he wylle drynke more in a houre

Than two men may gete in fowre;   152
When ʒe haue wrouʒht alle þat ʒe canne
Yit schalle he neuer be thryfty mane.'
    Than bespake þe polyff
With gret strong wordes & styffe: 156
'How, ser twyuet, me thinke ʒou greuyd;
What deuylle, who hath ʒou þus meuyd?
Thof he spend more in a ʒere
Off gold & syluer than þou may bere,   160
Y schall hym helpe with all my myght;
I trow to make hym ʒet a knyght.'
    'What, ser,' seyd þe wyndas rewle,
'Me thynke þou arte bot a fole,   164
Fore þou spekes oute of sesone;
He may not the þerfore by resone;
A carpenter to be a knyght?
That was euer ageyne ryght.   168
Therefore I schall telle þe a saw:
"Who-so wold be hyʒe he schall be law!"'
    'ʒe,' than seyd þe rewle stone,
'Mayster hath many fone;   172
And ʒe wold helpe hym at his nede
My mayster schuld þe better spede;
Bot what-so-euer ʒe brage ore boste,
My master ʒet schall reule þe roste;   176
Fore as I ame a trew mane
I schalle hym helpe all þat I canne.'
    The gowge seyd, 'þe deuyles dyrte
Fore any thyng þat thow canne wyrke!   180
Fore all þat euer þou canne do,
Yt is not worthe an old scho!
Thow hast be prentys þis vij ʒere
And ʒit thy crafte is forto lere;   184
And þou couthe wyrke als wele as he,
ʒet schall þi mayster neuer the!'
    'Softe, ser,' seyde þe gabulle rope,
'Me thinke gode ale is in ʒour tope;   188
Fore þou spekes as þou wold fyght,
There-to & þou hade any myght;
Y schall telle þe an oþer tale
My mayster how I schall aveyle;   192
Hayle & pulle I schall fulle faste
To reyse housys whyle I may laste,
And so within a lytell throw
My mayster gode schall not be know.'   196
    Than spake þe wryghtes wyfe:
'Noþer of ʒou schall neuer thryfe,
Noþer þe mayster ne þe mane,
Fore nothinge þe ʒe do canne;   200
Fore ʒe wyll spend in a moneth
More gode than iij men hath.'
    The squyre seyd, 'What sey ʒe dame?
ʒe schuld not speke my mayster schame!'   204
    'Squyre, I haue none oþer cause,
I suere þe by Seynt Eustase;

Fore alle þe ȝerne þat I may spynne
To spend at ale he thinkes no synne;   208
He wylle spend more in an owre
Than þou & I canne gete in fowre!'
   'Ȝit me thinke ȝe be to blame
To gyffe my master syche a name;   212
For thoff he spend more than ȝe haue
Yit his worschype ȝe schuld saue.'
   'Mary, I schrew hym & þe to
And alle them þat so canne do!   216
Fore hys seruaunt I trow þou be;
Therefore þou schalle neuer the;
Fore and þou lerne þat craft at hym
The thryft I trow schall be fulle thine.'   220
   The draught nayle þan spake he
And seyd, 'Dame, þat is no le;
ȝe hafe þe maner of þes frekes
That þus fore my mayster spekes;   224
Bot lythe to me a lytelle space,
Y schall ȝow telle all þe case
How þat they wyrke fore þer gode;
I wylle not lye, be þe rode.   228
When þei haue wroght an oure or two,
Anone to þe ale þei wylle go
And drinke þer whyle þei may dre,
"Thou to me" & "I to the!"   232
And seys, "þe ax schall pay fore þis;
Therefore þe cope ons I wylle kys,"
And when þei comme to werke ageyne
The belte to hys mayster wylle seyne,   236
"Mayster, wyrke no oute off resone;
The dey is vary longe of seson;
Smale strokes late vs hake
And sumtyme late vs es oure bake."   240
The wymbull spekes lyte: "A, syre,
Seuyne pens off a dey is smale hyre
Fore wryghtes þat wyrke so faste;
And in owre werke haue grete haste."   244
The groping iren seys full sone,
"Mayster, wylle ȝe wele done?
Late vs not wyrke to we suete
Fore cachyng of ouer gret hete;   248

Fore we may after cold to take,
Than on stroke may we no hake."
Than bespake þe whetstone
And seyd, "Mayster, we wylle go home   252
For faste it draw vnto þe nyght;
Oure soper by þis I wote is dyght."
The lyne & stone, þe persere & fyle
Seys, "þat is a gode counesylle."   256
The crow, þe pleyn, & þe squyre
Seys, "We haue arnyd wele oure hyre."
And þus with fraudes & falsyd
Ys many trew man deseyuid.   260
Therefore by ought þat I canne se
They schall neuer thryue ne the;
Therefore þe craft I wylle go froo
And to an oþer wylle I goo.'   264
   Than ansuerd þe wyfe in hye:
'And I myght, so wold I;
Bot I ame to hym bounde sa faste
That of my halter I may not caste;   268
Therefore þe preste þat bounde me prentys,
He schall treuly haue my curse
And euer schall haue to þat I dyȝe,
In what contre þat euer he be!'   272
   Therefore, wryȝtes, take hede of þis
That ȝe may mend þat is amysse,
And treuly þat ȝe do ȝour labore
Fore þat wylle be to ȝour honour.   276
And greue ȝou no-thinge at þis songe
Bot euer make mery ȝour-selue amonge;
Ne ȝet at hym þat it dud make,
Ne envy at hym ȝe take,   280
Ne none of ȝou do hym blame,
Fore-why the craft hath do hym schame
By mo weys than two or thre;
Thus seys þe boke, serteynlye.   284
   God þat is bothe gode & hend,
Gyff ȝou grace þat ȝe may mend
And bryng vs alle vnto his blysse,
That neuer fro vs schall mysse.   288
     Amen qd Rate

REFERENCES

Bettesworth, A., and Hitch, C. *The Builder's Dictionary*. 2 vols. London, 1734.

Carson, Cary, et al. "Impermanent Architecture in the Southern American Colonies." *Winterthur Portfolio* 10, no. ⅔ (1981).

Conlee, John. "Debate of the Carpenter's Tools." Unpublished typescript, 1986.

Diderot, Denis, et al. *Encyclopédie*. 17 vols. Paris, 1751–65.

Girard, Denis. *Cassell's French Dictionary*. New York: Funk and Wagnalls, 1962.

Goodman, W. L. *The History of Woodworking Tools*. London: G. Bell and Sons, 1964.

Hewitt, Cecil. *The Development of Carpentry 1200–1700: An Essex Study*. Newton Abbot, Devon: David and Charles, 1969.

Hindle, Brooke. *The Pursuit of Science in Revolutionary America 1735-1789*. New York: W. W. Norton and Co., 1956.

_____, ed. *America's Wooden Age*. Tarrytown, N.Y.: Sleepy Hollow Restorations, 1975.

Holtzapffel, Charles. *Turning and Mechanical Manipulation*. vol. 2. London: Holtzapffel, 1875.

Hulot. *L'art du tourneur mecanicien*. Paris: Roubo, 1775.

Hummel, Charles. *With Hammer in Hand*. Charlottesville: University Press of Virginia, 1968.

Jones, Michael Owen. *The Hand Made Object and Its Maker*. Berkeley: University of California Press, 1975.

Klemm, Friedrich. *A History of Western Technology*. New York: Charles Scribner's Sons, 1959.

Knight, Edward H. *Knight's American Mechanical Dictionary*. 3 vols. Boston: Houghton, Osgood and Co., 1880.

Mercer, Henry. *Ancient Carpenter's Tools*. Doylestown, Pa.: Bucks County Historical Society, 1929.

Moxon, Joseph. *Mechanick Exercises*. London, 1678.

Nicholson. *Mechanical Exercises*. London, 1816.

Noel Hume, Ivor. *Martin's Hundred*. New York: Alfred A. Knopf, 1982.

Nutting, Wallace. *Furniture of the Pilgrim Century*. New York: Crown Publishers, 1921.

Osborn, Susan. *American Rustic Furniture*. New York: Harmony Books, 1984.

Oxford English Dictionary. Oxford: Clarendon Press, 1933.

Perry, L. Day. *Seat Weaving*. Peoria: Chas. A. Bennett Co., 1940.

Phleps, Hermann. *The Craft of Log Building*. Karlsruhe, 1942. English-language edition, Ottawa, Ont.: Lee Valley Tools, Ltd., 1982.

Plumier, Charles. *L'art du tourner*. Lyon: Jean Certe, 1701.

Pollak, Emil and Martyl. *A Guide to American Wooden Planes and Their Makers*. Moristown: Astragal Press, 1983.

Roberts, Ken. *Wooden Planes in Nineteenth-Century America*. 3 vols. Fitzwilliam, New Hampshire: Ken Roberts Publishing Company, 1983.

Roubo, Andre-Jacob. *L'art du menuisier*. Paris, 1769–75.

Salamon, R. A. *Dictionary of Tools Used in the Woodworking and Allied Trades,
c. 1700–1970*. New York: Charles Scribner's Sons, 1975.

Salivet, Louis Georges Isaac. *Manuel du tourneur*. Paris: Bergeron, 1816.

Smith, Joseph. *Explanation or Key, to the Various Manufactories of Sheffield*. Sheffield: published by the author, 1816.

Tatham, William. *An Historical and Practical Essay on the Culture and Commerce of Tobacco*. London, 1800.

Viires, A. *Woodworking in Estonia*. Tallinn, 1960. English-language edition, National Technical Information Service, 1969.

INDEX